—————————A Review of—————————
# Private Approaches
—————————for Delivery of—————————
# Public Services

# A Review of
# Private Approaches
## for Delivery of
# Public Services

## Harry P. Hatry

*An Urban Institute Paperback*

 THE URBAN INSTITUTE PRESS · WASHINGTON, D.C.

A *Review of Private Approaches for Delivery of Public Services* is a slightly modified
version of *Alternative Service Delivery Approaches Involving Increased Use of the
Private Sector*. *Alternative Service Delivery* was first published in June 1983 by the
Greater Washington Research Center, Washington, D.C. That report was prepared
for the center's Task Force on Local Government Response to Fiscal Pressure.

Printed in the United States of America

**Library of Congress Cataloging in Publication Data**

Hatry, Harry P.
    A review of private approaches for delivery of public services.

    1. Municipal services—United States—Contract services.
    2. Local government—United States. I. Title.
HD4605.H383    1983        352.1'61'0973        83-23299
ISBN 0-87766-329-7

THE URBAN INSTITUTE is a nonprofit policy research and educational organization established in Washington, D.C. in 1968. Its staff investigates the social and economic problems confronting the nation and government policies and programs designed to alleviate such problems. The Institute disseminates significant findings of its research through the publications program of its Press. The Institute has two goals for work in each of its research areas: to help shape thinking about societal problems and efforts to solve them, and to improve government decisions and performance by providing better information and analytic tools.

Through work that ranges from broad conceptual studies to administrative and technical assistance, Institute researchers contribute to the stock of knowledge available to public officials and to private individuals and groups concerned with formulating and implementing more efficient and effective government policy.

Conclusions or opinions expressed in Institute publications are those of the authors and do not necessarily reflect the views of other staff members, officers or trustees of the Institute, or of any organizations which provide financial support to the Institute.

# CONTENTS

# EXHIBITS

# FOREWORD

As pressure to reduce the costs of government besieges local and state agencies, managers are forced to assess their governments' services, determining anew how these services should be delivered, and even whether a government should undertake certain activities at all. In response to these pressures, public managers may see greater use of the private sector as an attractive option. The private sector, it is argued, faces less red tape and through competition can be motivated to drive down costs and improve service quality. Furthermore, private firms working in more than one location can take advantage of economies of scale and are better able to develop superior management information systems.

This report focuses on the private sector's potential to help provide state and local government services. The author examines current options for service delivery involving increased use of the private sector. He reports on eleven different approaches, especially regarding their potential cost savings and service improvements. The author notes that in the future government managers will have to become more entrepreneurial. Information on this topic is still limited, but this report provides a useful, early analysis to those managers who have begun the search for new options.

William Gorham
*President*
The Urban Institute

# ACKNOWLEDGMENTS

This report was initially commissioned by the Greater Washington Research Center (GWRC) as a background paper for the Washington, D.C. Area Task Force on Local Government Response to Fiscal Pressures. Atlee E. Shidler, president of GWRC and Edwin T. Haefele of the University of Pennsylvania and research director for the task force played major roles in encouraging and reviewing the report.

Members of the Subgroup on Alternative Revenue Sources and Alternative Service Delivery Systems provided valuable advice and suggestions on the report. These include Phillip S. Hughes of the Smithsonian Institution; Vernon Ford of Arlington, Virginia; David E. McGiffert of Covington & Burling; Charles E. McKittrick of IBM; Walter A. Scheiber of the Metropolitan Washington Council of Governments; and John Shannon of the Advisory Commission on Intergovernmental Relations. Jacquelyn Perry of The Urban Institute and Janice Baker, GWRC, provided valuable assistance throughout the editorial process.

# ABOUT THE AUTHOR

HARRY P. HATRY is director of The Urban Institute's State and Local Government Research Program. He is widely known for his work as a principal contributor to a number of studies examining ways to improve the capability of state and local government agencies to deliver services. He has coauthored numerous publications, including *Practical Program Evaluation for State and Local Governments; How Effective Are Your Community Services?;* and *Obtaining Citizen Feedback: The Application of Citizen Surveys to Local Governments.* He holds a bachelor's degree from Yale University and a master's degree from Columbia University.

# CHAPTER 1

# INTRODUCTION

This report examines a number of options that local governments should consider as they revise their approaches to service delivery. We focus on those options that involve increased use of the private sector.[1]

The number of recent articles, books, and conference sessions devoted to alternative service delivery and the new jargon springing up (e.g., privatization, nonservice approaches, mediating structures, exit, private-public partnerships, load-shedding, coproduction, and voluntarism) indicate that this topic has become something of a fad.

Nevertheless, this phenomenon differs from recent fads in government management practices (such as zero-based budgeting, program budgeting, planning programming budgeting systems, and performance budgeting). Interest in alternative service delivery is driven by major fiscal changes, forcing public officials to consider many of the approaches described in this report.[2] Most of these approaches have already been used, to a limited extent, by local governments across the country. There is, however, danger that claims made for them will greatly exceed what they can accomplish and the ease with which they can be successfully used. Nevertheless, these new approaches to service delivery warrant serious attention by public officials.

# The New Approaches

This report briefly describes current options for service delivery, provides examples, and offers information on the impacts of these approaches, especially regarding significant cost savings and service improvements.

Individual jurisdictions may take a wide variety of actions, as listed in exhibit 1. (Definitions of these actions are provided in exhibit 2.)[3] These approaches can be used in various combinations and, when taken by local governments, produce at least one of the following consequences:

Provide a given service at lower cost

Reduce demand for service and thus lower government costs

Reduce the government service without reducing demand

Raise more revenues for government service

Increase the amount, quality, or effectiveness of the government service without increasing costs

Exhibit 1 shows which of these consequences is principally intended by each approach.

# Scope of This Report

This report focuses on alternatives to delivery of basic services by local government employees. Government activities such as development of the local economy, urban and housing renewal (including zoning), or the development of jobs are not considered.[4] These activities, however, have traditionally involved private-public interactions, and much of what is said here also likely applies to those activities. Also, this report only rarely draws examples from education. Elementary and secondary education, however, is a major local expense. Most of the discussion probably also applies to many educational activities.

Alternative revenue-raising options are not discussed except for fees and charges. Fees and charges, however, are discussed but only in regard to their capacity to affect the demand for services, not in their capacity to increase revenues.

This report concentrates on the eleven approaches listed above the double line in exhibit 1, those approaches that involve increased

---

Exhibit 1. ALTERNATIVE GOVERNMENT ACTIONS AND CONSEQUENCES

---

*Actions Involving Privatization*

Contract out—b

Give franchise(s)—c

Give a grant or subsidy to help someone else do it—c

Provide vouchers—c,e

Substitute volunteers for government employees—b

Encourage self-help/do-it-yourself—c

Alter regulations or tax policy—a

Encourage private agencies to take over an activity—c

Demarket/reduce the demand—a

Obtain temporary help from private firms (e.g., loaned executives)—b

Use fees and charges to adjust demand—a,d

---

Form joint public-private ventures—b

*Other Actions Not Involving Privatization*

Improve productivity of service activities—b

Cooperate, consolidate, or contract with other government entities—b

Form special, quasigovernmental agencies—d

Increase revenues such as taxes or fees and charges—d

Reduce level of service—c

---

**Consequences for Service Levels and Service Costs**

**a.** Reduce demand for the service and thus lower government cost.

**b.** Provide government service but at lower cost.

**c.** Reduce government service without reducing demand.

**d.** Raise more dollars for service.

**e.** Improve quality/responsiveness of service.

private sector participation. The approaches below the double line are also important but are beyond the scope of this paper. To put the approaches examined in this paper in better perspective, however, the following paragraphs briefly discuss each of these other areas.

As noted earlier, public-private joint ventures, such as a downtown redevelopment project, are major options to a government and are probably indispensable for certain types of projects. The private sector most often participates because of its business interests, not because of its purely community-spirited motivation. The government, because of its interest in the development of the community, provides a variety of assistance, including obtaining federal funds where available, using its regulatory and taxing authority, and providing selected services.[5]

Continuous attention to improve the internal productivity of government employee service delivery is certainly desirable. Though not likely to produce dramatic results, costs should be reduced. Some have estimated that a 10 percent reduction in cost across-the-board is probably about the maximum reduction to expect, but this may be higher for individual services. For example, a jurisdiction can substantially reduce its sanitation costs by reducing the size of solid waste collection crews from three to two persons.

Cost savings can be made by cooperating with, contracting with, or even consolidating activities with other governments, in such areas as data processing or purchasing. Savings are produced by achieving economies of scale, taking advantage of specialization, or reducing duplication of efforts.

Formation of special quasigovernmental agencies, such as water and sewer districts and transportation authorities, is likely to become more prevalent. Many districts have been established because of regional concerns, but now a major purpose is to insulate revenue raising for these specific services from the more political environment of general-purpose governments.

Of course, a government can also attempt to increase its revenues, for example, through property taxes, sales taxes, and fees and charges. The alternatives discussed here are attempts to avoid this option, which is beyond the scope of this report (except for fees and charges, to the extent they are used to adjust the demand for services).

Finally, a government can reduce costs by reducing the level of service—example, reducing the frequency of garbage collection, re-

Exhibit 2. DEFINITIONS OF ALTERNATIVE APPROACHES TO SERVICE
DELIVERY

1. *Contracting out/purchase of service.* The local government contracts with private firms (profit or nonprofit) to provide goods
   or deliver services. The local government may contract to have
   all, or a portion, of a service provided by the private firm. Contracting to other governmental bodies is discussed under Approach #14 below.

2. *Franchises.* The local government awards either an exclusive
   or nonexclusive franchise to private firms to provide a service
   within a certain geographical area. Under a franchise agreement, the citizen directly pays the firm for the service.

3. *Grants/subsidies.* The local government makes a financial or
   in-kind contribution to a private organization or individuals to
   encourage them to provide a service so that the government
   does not have to provide it.

4. *Vouchers.* The government provides vouchers to citizens needing the service. The citizens are then free to choose the organization from which to buy the goods or services. The citizen
   gives the voucher to the organization, which obtains reimbursement from the government.

5. *Volunteers.* Individuals in the jurisdictions provide free help to
   a government agency. For this report, this approach is limited
   to volunteers that work directly for a local government. It does
   not include individuals doing volunteer work for a private (e.g.,
   charitable) agency.

6. *Self-help.* The government encourages individuals or groups,
   such as neighborhood associations, to undertake for their own
   benefit, activities that the government has previously been undertaking. This results in a reduction in government activity
   that otherwise would be required.

---

Exhibit 2. (continued) DEFINITIONS OF ALTERNATIVE APPROACHES TO
SERVICE DELIVERY

---

7. *Use of regulatory and taxing authority.* The government uses
   its regulatory (deregulatory) or taxing authority to encourage
   members of the private sector (organizations or individuals) to
   provide a service or at least to reduce the need for public services.

8. *Encouragement of private organizations to take over an activity
   (service shedding).* Here the government actually gives up responsibility for an activity but works with a private agency
   (profit or nonprofit) willing to take over responsibility. (This
   might involve a one-time grant or subsidy.)

9. *Demarketing/reduce demand for service.* The government attempts to reduce the need and demand for a government service
   through a variety of marketing techniques.

10. *Obtaining temporary help from private firms.* Private firms loan
    personnel, facilities, or equipment, or even provide funds to the
    local government.

11. *User fees and charges to adjust demand.* Users of a service are
    charged a fee based on their amount of use of the government-
    supplied activity, thus putting the fiscal burden on users of the
    activity. This report is not concerned with the use of fees and
    charges for the sake of raising revenues.

---

12. *Joint public-private ventures.* Businesses in the community and
    the local government join forces for a major development, such
    as a new shopping mall or downtown revitalization project. Al-
    though this is a major type of private participation, this topic
    is not addressed in this report, which focuses on basic municipal
    services.

13. *Internal productivity improvements.* The government takes
    strictly internal actions to make better use of its existing re-
    sources—to reduce its costs for a given level of output or increase
    output (quantity or quality) for a given expenditure level. Nu-
    merous approaches to productivity improvement exist, such as

---

Exhibit 2. (continued)

use of new technology, employee motivational programs, changes in work methods, and organizational changes. This is a major topic, but it is not discussed in this report.

14. *Cooperation, consolidation, or contracting with other government units.* This can bring efficiencies by taking advantage of economies of scale and specialization. Since the approach does not involve use of the private sector, it is not discussed in this report.

15. *Formation of special, quasigovernment agencies.* Special water and sewer districts, transportation authorities, and park districts are used widely. They are not operated directly by elected officials and therefore are somewhat insulated from the political, bureaucratic, and other problems of local governments. Revenue can be raised with fewer obstacles. (For example, fees can be more readily set to cover full cost, capital as well as operating costs.) This approach, however, also insulates the service from public control and from the need to compete for funds against other public services. Since this approach does not involve the use of the private sector, it is not discussed further in this report. Officials of these quasigovernment bodies may want to consider some of the alternative approaches discussed in this report.

16. *Increase revenues.* Rather than attempting to reduce service levels or expenditures, a government can, of course, attempt to increase its revenues such as property taxes, sales taxes, fees and charges, or grants from other levels of government. This subject is outside the scope of this report.

17. *Reduction of service levels.* A major way to reduce cost is to reduce the amount of service provided, such as reducing the frequency of garbage collection, reducing library hours, or stretching out road repairs. This is a last resort but an action that is frequently taken these days.

---

NOTE: The definitions for (1)–(8) are based on those used by the International City Management Association in its examination of alternative delivery approaches.

ducing library hours, stretching out road repairs, cutting recreation programs, and reducing water quality standards. One of the messages of alternative delivery systems is that perhaps actions other than reducing service levels should be considered.

## Rationale for Alternatives

An important new philosophy is that city and county officials should take on a new role. Rather than act as service producers, local officials should become overseers, brokers, or facilitators concerned with the provision of services regardless of how they are delivered. Officials should consider a spectrum of alternatives to service delivery to carry out overall local government policy.

A major rationale for considering these alternatives is that local governments have held a monopoly in delivering services and therefore lack the motivation to reduce costs or improve performance. And those who believe there is excessive professionalism in government (especially in the human services) believe the professionals have produced additional service requirements, leading to additional costs not justified by the need or the desire of the community.[6]

A related major rationale is that the private sector can inherently do a better job of service delivery than the public sector can. The public sector has bureaucratic restrictions and rules and regulations that greatly limit the flexibility of local government managers. These include Civil Service regulations and living in a fishbowl atmosphere in which even lower-level government supervisors experience pressure from a wide variety of interest groups and service claimants; and the public sector lacks strong motivational incentives, such as the profit motive, which the private sector has. By cutting costs, private (for-profit) firms can increase their competitiveness and their profits.

There is another side to this story. As Mayor George Latimer of St. Paul has pointed out,

> The private sector also has had its problems in delivering expensive and desirable products: the private sector has had a decline in productivity, slackening investment in research and development, an unwillingness to consider external effects of private actions, a lack of capital investment, a trend to see short-term benefits, resistance to experiment with creative management, a loss of competitive strength when compared to foreign industry, and problems with the public sector

contracting out enormous sums of dollars to private businesses where we have seen delays, cost overruns, and sometimes frauds.[7]

To this can be added occasional bankruptcies and work stoppages. And, if private sector delivery is itself not handled so as to include effective competition, it may become a monopoly and lack motivation to achieve greater efficiency or maintain service quality.

In many local governments, agency managers have been under heavy pressure to cut back costs. Nevertheless, obstacles to modernization exist. Local legislatures are reluctant to provide funds to upgrade equipment and facilities if that means raising revenues. In many jurisdictions, local elected officials, hoping that competition will yield lower cost, find it more politically attractive to use such alternatives as contracting to private industry.

An additional popular rationale is the view that—regardless of cost and performance implications—less government is better and citizens should be able to make more choices for themselves rather than have public managers make choices for them. Although this view is partly a philosophical issue, it is also an appropriate question for systematic examination.

## Evaluating Alternatives

A key question for local governments considering alternative approaches is how well such approaches have worked in past trials. Unfortunately, little systematic, objective evaluation of most of these alternatives is available. Most available information is descriptive, anecdotal, and advocacy or public-relations oriented. Information on the consequences of the use of these approaches, when mentioned at all, is usually provided by the government that undertook the action, and such information is usually limited to assessments in the first year of the activity—before longer-term consequences have been identified. Estimates of cost savings that are provided are often estimates of expected savings. One, therefore, may have to rely on highly limited evidence and on personal judgments for evaluations. Nevertheless, it is vital that local governments carefully assess alternatives before making changes.

Local governments considering alternative approaches to service delivery should assess them relative to the current delivery practiced. The following criteria appear appropriate for evaluating each alternative approach. Individual communities should use criteria such as the following to select desirable approaches and, subsequently, to evaluate new approaches taken:

1. The cost of the government service
2. The financial cost to citizens
3. The degree of choices available to service clients
4. The quality/effectiveness of the service
5. The potential distributional effects
6. The staying power and potential for service disruption
7. Its feasibility (that is, ease of implementation)
8. Overall impact

Each criterion is discussed in the following pages.

**Cost of the Government Service.** Probably the predominant purpose of these alternatives is to reduce the cost of government services. Any approach should be assessed as to its potential for reducing the costs of government and the potential size of that reduction. In this analysis, governments need to consider administrative costs associated with individual approaches, such as for monitoring contracts or finding and coordinating volunteers.

**Financial Cost to Citizens.** Closely related to the governmental cost is the resulting financial cost to citizens. Some arrangements, such as increased use of fees and charges and tax credits, permit some citizens to reduce their costs. But there may be added service costs to clients. For example, privatization of a service may lead to a monopoly, and the cost to clients may become higher than under government delivery. Switching to franchises can substantially reduce a government's costs but may have much smaller effects on costs to clients.

**Choices Available to Citizens.** A second purpose sometimes identified for alternatives is to provide more choices to citizens. Each approach and specific application should be assessed for its ability to provide citizens with improved choices of suppliers and service levels. This applies particularly to the use of nonexclusive franchises, vouchers, deregulation, use of fees and charges, and arrangements in which neighborhoods or individuals are given increased responsibility for service selection.

**Quality and Effectiveness of the Service.** Applications of these alternate approaches will likely have consequences for the quality and effectiveness of the service. These should be explicitly considered. A related concern, as the American Federation of State, County and Municipal Employees has fervently pointed out, is that private (for-profit) sector delivery can lead to a greater amount of fraud and corruption.[8] On the other hand, use of self-help and volunteers may encourage more community spirit and a greater sense of self-satisfaction. Private, for-profit firms may increase the quality of the service to meet competition.

**Potential Distributional Effects.** Distributional effects can result. Each approach should be assessed as to its potential for causing distributional problems and the need to compensate some groups. For each application, who gains? Who loses? Are some groups affected detrimentally (or beneficially) compared to others? If so, can (and should) they be compensated in some way? If some form of compensation is needed, this could cause added government costs. A major concern is whether low-income families are likely to be adversely affected, for example, if fees and charges are introduced.

**Staying Power and Potential for Service Disruption.** Approaches should be evaluated as to their staying power and potential for service disruption. Can the program be sustained? Will it last? How likely is it that sufficient competition will continue to avoid a contractor monopoly? Will volunteers continue to be available? Will private organizations be likely to continue service delivery, such as operation of a hospital? Service disruptions are more likely for some approaches than others. For example, strikes and bankruptcies by a private business can occur. Strikes or slowdowns by local government employees also occur but probably less frequently. A related question is the extent to which an approach is reversible. If it does not work or if the private agency withdraws, can the decision be reversed without sustained cost? If a government gets out of a service completely, including giving up all its facilities and equipment, the approach is, of course, very difficult. If part of the service is still performed by government workers or if some facilities and equipment are still owned by a government, reversal of the approach would be easier to achieve. Governments should consider the possibilities of disruption when evaluating these approaches and may want to provide for such contingencies by retaining at least a small delivery capability.

**Feasibility.** Each approach and each application will have its own set of feasibility issues and ease of implementation. Such issues include the amount of time and effort needed to sell and implement the approach; the legal constraints; the need for modifications of existing state laws or local ordinances; the personnel questions; and the extent and nature of resistance by various interest groups in the community. Most of the approaches can have substantial political implications for elected officials. Inevitably, some community interest groups will oppose any particular action.

**Overall Impact.** This criteria summarizes the findings to date on the overall impact of an approach. In chapters 2 through 12, each of the eleven approaches is examined against each of the preceding criteria.

## Other Issues

The applicability of alternative approaches will vary somewhat among specific services. For example, recreation and library services have made frequent use of volunteers to help with special recreation programs and to serve as library aides. Many citizens like to work in libraries and in recreation programs. On the other hand, volunteers have been infrequently used in public works programs, such as street maintenance and water and sewer services. The latter jobs are clearly dirtier and do not appeal to public volunteers; also, some of the tasks require special skills or hard physical work.

Policy makers considering different approaches should be aware that the effectiveness of these approaches depends very much on particular conditions in the jurisdiction, on the quality of the implementation, and on maintenance of that quality in subsequent years. Experience with a variety of productivity improvement efforts in local governments indicates that even the best of intentions and the best of ideas can be thwarted by inadequate and inappropriate actions, both during initial implementation and subsequently.

# CHAPTER 2

# CONTRACTING OUT

## Definition and Rationale

In contracting out, the local government contracts with private firms (profit or nonprofit) to provide goods or deliver services. The local government may contract to have all or a portion of the service provided by the private firms. Contracting with other governments or special districts (such as a city contracting for police services from its county) is not considered here since this arrangement does not involve a private organization.

The major purpose for contracting with the private sector is to reduce costs. The assumption is that private firms are able to deliver the service at lower cost than the government agency can. Private firms have more incentive to keep costs down, especially if there is competition for the contracts among potential suppliers. Private firms also can avoid the bureaucratic problems inherent in local governments. Private firms may have lower employee compensation costs. (This is a relatively recent development; until the mid-1970s, local government employee compensation was quite low.) In addition, for-profit firms that serve many communities are more likely to be able and motivated to explore and experiment with newer technology and new procedures. Individual governments are less likely to have the time or incentive to undertake even limited research and development or experimentation.

Another major reason for contracting, though of less interest in this report, is to meet a temporary need for assistance or an intermittent need for highly specialized help. In those cases, it is not practical for governments to provide a full-time internal capability.

An important element for lower costs through contracting is competition among potential service providers. If only one or very few suppliers are available, the major advantage of contracting may be lost.

Contracting has several potential drawbacks. The government gives up some direct control over service delivery. Many argue that for-profit firms will concentrate on cutting costs to the detriment of the level and quality of service. Also, service interruptions are more likely because of possible financial failure of the business or labor stoppages and slowdowns. In addition, the for-profit firm needs to make a profit, and the cost charged to the govenment agency will include that added cost. Finally, the introduction of the profit motive can bring with it corruption.

## Variations in Contracting

A number of important variations in contracting have appeared in recent years. Governments have tried to stimulate competition by splitting the jurisdiction into districts with firms competing for each district. This permits more, smaller-size organizations to compete. Some local governments have divided the work into segments, with some work allocated to the public agency and other work distributed to private contractors. In a more unusual approach, some governments have begun to provide direct competition between the local government's own agency and private firms. The public agency bids on jobs in direct competition with the private bidders.

A side benefit of splitting the market is that governments can reduce their vulnerability to job actions by contractors' personnel or to financial failure by the contractor. By retaining some delivery capability in an on-going agency, the government can intervene to provide the service if the contractor is unable to do so.[1]

There are also variations in the form of the contracts, variations intended to provide other incentives to contractors such as performance and incentive contracting. In these forms the contract specifies performance levels or provides rewards or penalties for meeting, exceeding, or not meeting performance targets. These variations enable the government to hold providers more accountable for performance on service quantity, quality, and timeliness. Local governments, however, can also use such practices internally by establishing performance targets (as in management-by-objectives programs) and by linking compensation of individual government employees to performance against targets. These practices are gaining wider application. Their use in government, however, is more difficult than in the private sector where there are fewer obstacles (e.g., Civil Service regulations) and where performance measurement (e.g., profits) is much easier.

A mid-1970s study identified the following advantages and disadvantages for contracting.[2]

## Advantages

May cost less or provide better performance

Provides specialized skills

Limits the growth of government

Avoids large initial costs

Permits greater flexibility in adjusting program size

Provides a yardstick for comparison[3]

Produces better management

## Disadvantages

May cost more

May result in poor service to citizens

May increase the chance of corruption

Raises the possibility that a contractor may not complete operations

Displaces public employees and draws opposition from municipal unions

Raises problems in drawing up adequate contracts

May be restricted by law

May entail problems in enforcing public policy

Fails to guarantee adequate competition for certain contracts

A May 1981 survey by the California Tax Foundation found a similar list of advantages and disadvantages. Exhibit 3 summarizes the advantages, disadvantages, and problems as reported by eighty-seven California local governments.[4]

---

Exhibit 3. ADVANTAGES AND DISADVANTAGES OF CONTRACTING OUT

*Summary of Advantages, Disadvantages, and Problems*

| *Responding entities* | *Cities* *(39)* | *Counties* *(19)* | *School Districts* *(17)* | *Special Districts* *(12)* |
|---|---|---|---|---|
| *Advantages of contracting out* | | | | |
| Reduced cost of labor, material, or overhead | 30 | 12 | 9 | 9 |
| Improve service | 16 | 7 | 7 | 6 |
| Ease in measuring/monitoring contractor performance | 9 | 6 | 1 | 5 |
| Ease in adjusting program size | 29 | 9 | 1 | 7 |
| Avoidance of start-up costs required to provide services | 25 | 10 | 7 | 8 |
| Availability of special equipment and skilled personnel | 28 | 13 | 15 | 10 |
| Prevents reduction in the level of service | 1 | — | 1 | 1 |
| Contractor absorbs political and public relations problems | 2 | — | — | 1 |
| Flexibility in contractor selection | 3 | — | — | — |
| Objectivity of contractor | 1 | 2 | 1 | 1 |
| Eliminates training costs for specialized activities | 1 | — | — | 1 |

Exhibit 3. (continued)

*Summary of Advantages, Disadvantages, and Problems*

| Responding entities | Cities (39) | Counties (19) | School Districts (17) | Special Districts (12) |
|---|---|---|---|---|
| *Disadvantages of contracting out* | | | | |
| Increased costs | 6 | 3 | 3 | 3 |
| Poorer service | 6 | 2 | 4 | 4 |
| Difficulty in monitoring contract | 19 | 8 | 2 | 4 |
| Displacement of employees | 5 | 3 | 1 | 1 |
| Unreliability of contractor | 11 | 8 | 3 | 7 |
| Contractor's insensitivity to citizen problems | 1 | — | — | — |
| Legal mandate to accept low bid | 1 | — | — | — |
| *Problems encountered in contracting out services* | | | | |
| Legislative constraints | 6 | 6 | 6 | 4 |
| Union or other employee organizations | 7 | 4 | 4 | 3 |
| Public to be served | 8 | 3 | 1 | 1 |
| Establishing contract cost when only one provider available | 1 | — | — | — |
| Difficulty in providing flexibility for extra-cost/services | 1 | 1 | — | 1 |
| Avoiding inferior service contracts (specification preparation) | — | 1 | 1 | 1 |
| Internal procedures | — | 1 | — | 1 |

SOURCE: California Tax Foundation, "Contracting Out Local Government Services in California," p. 9, May 1981.

## Examples

There is no lack of examples. Governments have been contracting for many years. Contracting for some services is quite common, such as solid waste collection, road construction, building construction, and a large variety of engineering and legal tasks.

In recent years, because of state fiscal containment efforts there has been a surge of contracting efforts. Fiscal containment legislation has made contracting both more tempting and easier for local governments. Also, the relatively new and important competitive types of contracting just described have come into use. Finally, governments are making a much more concerted effort to look at a variety of services to order to identify contracting opportunities.

Probably every local government of any size undertakes some contracting out. The focus in the examples given here is on unusual applications and those that involve substantial amounts of service activity.

- Orange County, California, has contracted its complete data processing services since about 1975. It has reported approximately $10 million annual savings. Prince George's County, Maryland, in 1981 entered into a similar contract for the first year and reported 14 percent savings. The city of San Diego in 1979 formed a private nonprofit corporation to manage its data processing. The board is from the private sector but appointed by the City Council. It possesses the normal authority of a business enterprise. (Here, however, there is no built-in competition.)[5]

- A number of local governments have contracted the management of hospitals. Between 1973 and October 1980, fifteen of California's thirty-nine county hospitals contracted with private management firms to administer public hospitals. However, also during this period, seven counties terminated their contracts, leaving eight California county hospitals operating under private management contracts as of October 1980.[6] The larger counties, those over 300,000 population, tended to be those that terminated the contracts. Alameda County was the largest with a population of about 1,100,000.

  The University of California at Los Angeles study of these contracts found no significant overall cost savings or quality changes but found significant gains in revenues from better accounting and billing systems and better handling of reimbursements from the state and federal governments. The hospital management firms concentrated on revenues rather than on expenditures.

Inner-city populations in the large counties offered considerable opposition to the hospital contracts. They expressed fear that service levels would lessen if private management continued. Public employee associations were also heatedly against the contracts. Another reason given for termination, especially for small jurisdictions, was that the public hospitals had no further need for the private firms, having learned their management techniques. However, a 1980 survey of hospital board members in seventy-eight government hospitals across the nation found a high level of satisfaction with their management contracts.[7]

- Scottsdale, Arizona (population of 95,000), and other cities in Arizona are well known for having contracted out to the Rural/Metro Fire Department, Inc. The company has served Scottsdale for more than twenty-five years. City employees are trained for part-time emergency calls to supplement the full-time paid employees. The company has reported fire service costs of approximately $17 per capita compared to a national average of more than double this sum for commodities of comparable size.[8] Two separate studies of the Scottsdale private fire department found strong evidence that the cost per capita was significantly below that which otherwise would have been expected.[9]

- In Denmark the private Falck Company has contracts with 271 of 279 municipalities for at least one service, particularly municipal fire and ambulance. It also uses paid reservists to supplement full-time personnel.[10]

- In Switzerland, 30 villages and towns ranging from a population of a few hundred to several thousand have contracted with Securitas, a private firm, for patrol services, and these villages and towns report substantial savings.[11]

- Pomona, California, has contracted out public defender work. The contractor works on a fixed hourly rate with a ceiling on total payments depending on case volume. In the first eight months of the current one-year pilot project the average cost per case was $205 versus $800 the previous year. The presiding judge reports that quality is at a high professional level.[12]

- Gainesville, Florida, in 1980 began contracting all its vehicle repair work. Former city employees filled the positions. The city estimated cost savings of 20 percent and reported lower vehicle downtime and fewer repeat repairs.[13]

- Social services agencies throughout the United States commonly have purchase-of-service contracts. Recently, their use has become more frequent to handle added caseload volume in the face of budget restrictions, to prevent government expansion, and to obtain donated funds to provide the match for federal reimbursement under Title XX. However, in the social services, most contracts are with nonprofit agencies, and there appears to be little competitive bidding. A study of contracting by the state of Massachusetts did not find any formal competitive procedures in the state agencies responsible for protective services for children, elderly affairs, or vocational rehabilitation (all three of the services covered in the study).[14]

- Both the state of California and the state of Texas have tried competitive contracting for selected social services. In California, the Office of Child Development (in the Department of Education) has an extensive request-for-proposal competition for child care services with each program being scored by a number of reviewers. Most bidders, but not all, are nonprofit organizations. The Texas effort is patterned after that of California. Beginning in late 1981, Texas began a trial of competitive contracting for day care, family care, family planning, and medical transportation. Neither state, however, has made cost a significant part of the competition. The competition is primarily on program characteristics.

- The state of Kentucky since 1975 has contracted the management and operation of its Outwood Mental Retardation facility to a for-profit firm. The state budget office recently reported that the facility has the lowest per diem cost of Kentucky's three comparable mental retardation facilities, and its per diem costs after deducting revenues have dropped from $32 to approximately $10.

- The Illinois Department of Corrections is contracting operation of eight of the state's twenty community correctional
  centers (CCCs) to nonprofit organizations, for example, the
  Salvation Army. These are work release centers. The department reported in 1982 that the cost per inmate day in
  private centers was $25 as compared to almost $40 in state-
  run CCCs (a 37 percent reduction). The Council of State Governments (CSG) in its examination of the program could find
  no discernible differences in employment rates or percentage
  of residents returned to prisons. An explanation for the cost
  savings, cited by CSG, was that the private nonprofit organizations receive private contributions, thus defraying some
  of the program costs.[15]

- LaMirada, California (41,000), a suburb of Los Angeles and
  a city formed in 1960, currently has fewer than sixty employees. But it has more than sixty contracts. Some contracts
  are with the county, such as police and fire, but most are with
  private for-profit firms. The contracts cover such services as
  data processing, traffic signal maintenance, park maintenance, refuse pickup, recreation, and a variety of human services, such as counseling, employment development, legal
  counseling, and some probation services. The city reports that
  it has greater control over private contractors than over the
  city departments.[16]

- The city of Poughkeepsie, New York, in 1979 contracted for
  operation of its wastewater treatment plant. Standards for
  various effluent characteristics, such as BOD and suspended
  solids, were included in the contract. The basic monthly compensation is increased or decreased annually according to
  changes in the consumer price index, the wholesale price index for electrical power, the wholesale price for industrial
  chemicals, and the prices for fuel oil. The contract is for five
  years and is renewable. The employees' union offered considerable resistance. The city projected cost savings for contracting to be approximately $250,000 a year, a reduction of
  approximately 25 percent.[17]

Besides these examples of basic contracting, there are also examples of innovations to increase the level of competition in contracting, or at least to increase the incentives for good performance
for those awarded contracts:

- Phoenix, Arizona, requires city agencies to bid along with private contractors for selected city contracts. The City Auditor's office prepares the city's bids. Services have included custodial services, trash and garbage collection, and street landscaping. In some cases, contracts are citywide; in others they are for service in specific locations in the city. The city agency may win the contract in some locations and the private contractor in others. For example, awards are made on a geographical basis for landscape maintenance service. Another example is Phoenix's 1980 request for proposal for uncontained refuse collection. The city was divided into five sectors, and bidders were allowed to bid on any combination of individual sectors or for the total city. Sealed bids were received from two private firms and from the city itself. The city won the contract in three of the areas and a private firm in the other two. From a total of twenty-two contracts in recent years, city forces have submitted the lowest bid ten times.[18]

- In Minneapolis, there are two intermixed service areas. In one, the private firm picks up solid waste and in the other, the public agency does. The characteristics of these areas are similar. Their unit cost has also been quite similar. The latter appears to be the result of a determined effort by city officials to drive down the costs of municipal collection so that it matches the low cost of contract collection.[19]

- Rochester, New York, was on the verge of contracting out waste collection for one sector of the city. On the eve of the contract signing, the public employees' union proposed that it could do it less expensively if the city reduced the crew size from four to three. This was an offer the city could not and did not refuse.[20]

- Montgomery County, Maryland, in 1978 divided its urban refuse collection district of 59,000 households formerly served by a single private contractor into nine districts, each serving between 6,000 and 10,000 households. Competitive bidding among private firms to serve the smaller districts has reduced the cost per household from $103 in 1978 to $88 in 1981, a 15-percent drop during a period of 26-percent inflation.[21]

- Tulsa, Oklahoma, in 1979 introduced an innovative contracting arrangement for solid waste collection that contains financial penalties if the haulers do not resolve complaints within 24 hours, if trash containers are not returned to their original location, if the lids are not replaced, or if the haulers do not pick up spilled trash. The contract also permits the city to take possession of all the contractor's equipment and facilities used in performance of the contract if the contractor fails to provide services required by the agreement for a period exceeding five consecutive working days.[22]

- The state of Kentucky's contract for management and operation of one of its mental retardation facilities (cited earlier) includes a cost-savings sharing provision. The latest contract provides a sliding scale with larger shares going to the contractor for the first 13 percent, a greater share of the savings between 13 and 15 percent, and no added amount to the contractor for cost savings above 15 percent of the contractor target.

- School districts engaged in a series of performance contracting experiments in the early 1970s. Private firms contracted to educate pupils. The firms' payments were based on gains in standardized reading tests and other measures. Many of these projects were funded by the U.S. Office of Economic Opportunity, which eventually reached a pessimistic conclusion about the value of the approach. By and large, the initial findings showed no significant improvements relating to performance contracting. Critics of the program pointed out that time was insufficient to properly test the approach, especially for such a radical departure from current practice.[23]

The preceding examples involve primarily for-profit firms. There are also contracts that involve nonprofit private agencies. These almost always, however, involve less competitive arrangements. There is a presumption that their costs may be less than if government employees were used, because nonprofit firms use lower-cost employees, volunteers, and donations from other sources. Two examples outside the social service field are as follows:

- The Hesperia Recreation and Park District in California, when Proposition 13 reduced its budget by 37 percent, entered into a unique contract with the local YMCA. The YMCA agreed to provide recreation services in district facilities to all Hesperian residents. The contract specifies that the district provides office space, pays most utility bills, and performs regular maintenance and repair. The YMCA responsibilities include providing and promoting all recreation programs and obtaining liability coverage for them. All programs are designed to be self-supporting and are billed as cosponsored. The district estimates that this arrangement saves $60,000 annually, permits more programs to be offered to more people, and provides stronger justification for continued maintenance funding.[24]

● Seattle, since 1974, has contracted with neighborhood associations and other established community groups for partial maintenance of vest-pocket parks. At any one time the Department of Parks and Recreation contracts with about seven groups maintaining fifteen parks. The groups themselves negotiate with neighborhood residents for performance of specific tasks. The dollars budgeted to this program buy more hours of maintenance than could be performed by city staff for the same money. The park department is careful to select community groups already set up to supervise and handle paperwork.[25]

## Evaluation

Contracting has probably been the most closely examined approach to privatization. The amount of independent, comprehensive evaluation of the effects of contracting, however, is quite small except for solid waste collection. Few trials of contracting, including the recent innovations, have been adequately evaluated to permit agencies nationally to learn under what conditions contracting works well.

**Cost of Government Service.** The evidence to date suggests that contracting can reduce the cost of government services more often than not. Studies of solid waste collection and fire control have found that local governments contracting to private firms tend to have costs at least 25 percent less than local governments where there is municipal delivery (but the evidence on fire control is limited to only a few local governments). The California hospital study, however, did not find cost savings.

The fire control evidence was discussed earlier. The evidence on solid waste collection primarily comes from two studies, one by Columbia University and the other by Yale University.[26] The first was a national cross-sectional comparison of about 315 local communities using a variety of delivery systems, and the second was an examination of about 130 Connecticut communities. Both found that communities contracting out had lower costs than those where municipal agencies delivered the service, about 25 percent less. The Columbia University study found that this primarily applied to local governments with populations over 50,000. (The highest costs occurred in communities where collection was completely private, with households dealing directly with private contractors. This is discussed further under "Franchises.")

The California Tax Foundation's 1981 survey of California local governments (cited previously) gives some qualitative, subjective substantiation to these findings and for other services as well. As indicated in exhibit 3, a substantially greater number of local governments reported that contracting had reduced their costs as distinct from increasing their costs (forty-two cities and counties versus nine).[27]

The Urban Institute's earlier study (cited previously) found more ambiguous evidence, which suggested that a shift in either direction, either from municipal to private or from private to municipal, would likely lead to reduced costs. The rationale is that when a local government is willing to make such a substantial shift, its previous condition is likely to be so inefficient that any change would lead to an improvement.

Contracting entails substantial administrative costs. Costs are necessary to implement the contracting process and to monitor the contracts. Unfortunately, the size of these costs has seldom been identified. A number of government officials have recently emphasized the critical need for careful monitoring of contractors' performance. These same officials have also indicated that for contract control, specific performance specifications in the contract itself are also needed.

Cost comparisons between municipal delivery and contracting out should also consider the other support and overhead costs associated with municipal delivery. How much of these can actually be saved if the service is contracted out? Again, the size of such costs has generally not been identified. Sometimes the nonprofit organization subsidizes its contract effort through its other funding sources.

This offsets what generally has been noncompetitive bidding, at least on cost, in the use of nonprofit organizations.

**Cost to Citizens.** Costs to citizens should be similar to the net cost savings from contracting (after netting out administrative costs). Thus, it appears that contracting can lead to somewhat reduced costs to citizens for contracted services. There are, however, cases where both government costs and costs to citizens will rise. This is likely to be the case where real competition among private firms is not maintained. Another problem is the possibility of corruption—because of the profit motive. A number of such incidents have been documented in a report published by the American Federation of State, County and Municipal Employees.[28]

**Choices Available to Clients.** Generally, contracting does not significantly alter the choices available to clients (though it gives more options to the government agency doing the contracting). There are exceptions, such as that noted earlier in the Hesperia Park District where the contract with the YMCA resulted in more recreational programs.

**Quality/Effectiveness of Service.** Because of the profit motive, contracts with for-profit firms may encourage cost reduction at the expense of service quality. The quality issue has received much less study than cost. The studies of solid waste collection have not directly addressed the problem of service quality, but the level of service, such as frequency of collection and whether it is back-door or curbside, is considered when making cost comparisons. Do private, for-profit employees deliver as high a level of service as government employees would? This is largely an unanswered question.

The California hospital study found no evidence that contract management had reduced or increased the quality of care.[29] In the case of performance contracting in education, aimed at improving education, the results were disappointing. There is no documented evidence yet from the Tulsa incentive contract experience. But with incentive contracting, contractors can be rewarded for meeting or exceeding quality standards; thus, quality probably can at least be controlled. Incentive contracting in local governments, however, is largely untested.

On the whole, local governments need to be concerned about potential reduction in quality in their attempt to achieve reduced costs from contracting. Contracts should at least include quality and quantity standards for the work to be performed.

**Distributional Effects.** With this approach, no clear-cut, generalizable distributional effects appear to exist. As the California hospital example indicates, however, there are situations where certain groups could find their service level at risk. The contract could, however, be worded to reduce this possibility.

**Staying Power and Potential for Service Disruption.** Shifting to contracting for at least some major activities is a major move and is not easy to reverse. The use of private contracting increases the possibility of service disruption. Private firms can go bankrupt or otherwise have severe financial problems, and they are more susceptible to work slowdown and stoppage than the public sector. Some have advised that large cities reduce their vulnerability to these problems by creating a system in which the local government retains a partial delivery capability and thus can step in if the private firm is unable to provide the service for short or long periods of time.[30] Governments can reverse contracting with some effort— and have, as indicated in the example of contracting the management of public hospitals.

**Feasibility.** Prior to recent state fiscal containment measures, shifting to contracting a service was quite difficult. It inevitably meant major resistance by the public employee unions and client groups in the community. Many proposals for contracting were not passed by city council, due to employee pressure and the concern that the quality of the service would diminish, particularly where for-profit firms are involved.

Fiscal austerity makes contracting easier, but resistance is still likely to be strong. Major struggles have occurred recently in Florida and Massachusetts over attempts to contract out state mental illness facilities. The unions have won the argument in some instances, the state in others. The union recently won a major victory in the state of Washington when the State Supreme Court upheld the union's position that contracting such services as custodial services in state institutions of higher learning violated the state's Personnel law.

Legal issues can inhibit or prevent contracting. This depends on current laws and ordinances at both the state and local levels on the legality of switching a service from government to private sector delivery.

More recently, especially in California, contracting has sprouted as resistance has fallen in the face of major revenue shortages.

**Overall Impact.** A broad spectrum of services, even fire control, have used contracting. However, in large jurisdictions, public safety operations such as police and fire departments have not been heavily involved in contracting. Other activities such as maintenance activities, data processing, and recreation have been the subject of major contracting activity. A key issue is whether sufficient firms exist in the jurisdiction to provide a competitive environment. Where this is the case, cost reductions of perhaps 25 percent or more seem possible.

However, it also seems quite possible that if government employees are given the opportunity to meet private competition, such as in Minneapolis and Rochester, or, as in Phoenix, to compete directly against the private sector for specific work, they also can achieve substantial and similar levels of savings. Such procedures introduce incentives that are otherwise lacking for government agencies.

These experiences suggest that governments should review services periodically, such as every two, three, or four years. If after careful cost comparisons, there appear to be significant potential savings from contracting, the government agency should have the opportunity to compete, either by giving the agency the opportunity to improve its performance or by having it compete directly with the private sector for work. Contracting arrangements that encourage competition, such as splitting the market into districts with competition for each district, and permitting the government agency to compete against firms, seem worthy and likely to provide incentives to reduce costs.

# CHAPTER 3

# FRANCHISES

## Definition and Rationale

With franchises, the local government awards either an exclusive or nonexclusive franchise to private firms to provide a service within a certain geographical area.[1] Individual citizens directly pay the firm for the service they receive. The government in effect has primarily a regulatory role. The government may or may not control the prices that private firms can charge or the service levels provided. Some form of public price control is usually imposed to avoid exploitation. Government control often also includes some service standards and requirements to serve all customers within the area of the franchise. Price and service regulations may be administered through a utility commission, an administrative bureau, or a local legislature. In exclusive franchises, the regulatory body establishes the rates. Rate making is generally based on an analysis of the firm's cost. As a rule, rates are set to allow the firm a fair rate of profit.

The primary rationale for franchising is that the government completely removes itself from the delivery business in favor of presumably more efficient private firms. In nonexclusive franchises, the franchised firms function in a competitive environment with customers able to choose among multiple suppliers. This continuing competition is intended to be a strong encouragement to improve efficiency, lower costs, and provide quality service to customers.

With nonexclusive franchises, clients should reasonably be expected to know what type of service they need, obtain relevant information on suppliers, and be able to evaluate the service delivered. If these elements do not exist, the added choice may backfire.

Where franchises are exclusive but come up for renewal at frequent intervals and are competitively awarded (e.g., exclusive solid waste collection franchises) they should, as in "Contracting Out," provide incentives for low-cost, quality service.

Licensing is a very similar approach, but licensing arrangements usually do not involve limiting the number of firms or individuals, as do franchises. Also, there are generally fewer controls (such as price controls) on licenses than on franchises. For the purposes here, licensing can be considered a related option for a local government—to permit private sector involvement with only a small amount of government control.

## Examples

Although there are not many existing applications of franchising, where franchising is used, it plays a major role in service delivery. The primary examples of existing franchises include electric power (exclusive franchises), taxi service (multiple franchises), solid waste collection (either type), emergency ambulance service (either type), and special recreational facilities such as golf course pro shops (exclusive).

Franchising in solid waste collection is common in small jurisdictions. A 1975 survey found that approximately 12 percent of cities with populations between 25,000 and 99,999 had franchises.[2] (Approximately 14 percent contracted for the service, 40 percent used municipal employees, and the remainder used some other form of completely private or self-service collection.) However, only 1 of 133 cities over 100,000 reported a franchise.

St. Paul has *licensed* a number of companies to do curb replacement directly for citizens, who can take out permits from the city to replace their curbs.[3] Theoretically, franchising (or licensing) can be used in any instance where contracting can be used, if the service is provided to identifiable, individual clients and is not a collective, inseparable service (so that the firm can charge for the particular type and amount of service given to the individual clients). Exhibit 4 indicates for selected local government services whether services are primarily provided to individuals, thus making those services the most likely candidates for franchising.

---

Exhibit 4. INDIVIDUAL VERSUS COLLECTIVE SERVICES (INDIVIDUAL SERVICES ARE MORE APPLICABLE TO FRANCHISING, VOUCHERS, AND FEES AND CHARGES)

| *Service* | *Service Provided to Individuals* | *Service Provided to Customers Who Require Financial Assistance*[c] | *Collectively Provided Services* |
|---|---|---|---|
| Police | | | x |
| Fire | | | x |
| Emergency ambulance | Partly[a] | | Partly[a] |
| Solid waste collection | x | | |
| Solid waste disposal | x | | |
| Street repair, traffic engineering/street lighting | | | x |
| Buses/public transit | x | | |
| Water and sewer | x | | |
| Recreation programs | x | | |
| Parks | x[b] | | |
| Libraries | x | | |
| Human services to low-income families | | x | |
| Inspections (building, housing, food, etc.) | Partly[a] | | Partly[a] |
| Support services (vehicle and building maintenance, electronic data processing, etc.) | | | x |

a. Part of the service can be considered as providing a standby capability helpful to all citizens, even though only a small percentage of the population may actually be served.

b. With large parks, however, collecting fees presents major problems for these approaches.

c. Franchises and full fees and charges are not likely to be appropriate, but vouchers are.

## Evaluation

**Cost of Government Service.** By switching to franchising, the government gets out of the delivery business, thereby substantially reducing its costs. The persons being served pay private suppliers directly. Somewhat offsetting this reduced cost to the government is the cost of monitoring the franchising operation. This cost, however, is likely to be small compared to the cost of delivery.

**Cost to Citizens.** Some empirical evidence exists in the field of solid waste collection, where private collection has been compared to collection by municipal employees and contracting. These studies found that private collection costs substantially more than either municipal or contract collection, roughly 25 percent–50 percent more than municipal collection, and even more when compared to contract collection.[4] These numbers unfortunately combine franchising and other forms of purely private collection.

One examination, however, did separate them.[5] It found franchises more expensive than contract or municipal collection but less expensive than fully private collection for once-a-week curbside collection ($27.94 annual cost per household for franchises versus $22.42, $24.41, and $35.91 for contracting, municipal delivery, and private collection, respectively). Franchises were also more expensive than both municipal and contract collection for twice-a-week curbside collection, but franchises were the least expensive mode for once-a-week backyard collection. For the latter two service levels, however, the sample sizes for franchise cities were quite small, fewer than ten cities.

Two major issues are the extent to which entry by private firms is restricted and the extent to which the local government regulates price. These factors can greatly affect the actual costs to the service recipients and determine whether their direct payments to the franchised providers will be less or more than the government's charges or taxes for the service. Exclusive franchises in general will be heavily regulated as to rates. The local government typically bases its rate determination on an analysis of the firm's costs, with a fair rate of profit added. It is likely that such rates will be higher than the rate that the local government would charge. It is easier politically for private firms to increase rates than for local governments to do so. And the private firm will expend effort to sell to the public any rate increases. If entry is severely restricted (e.g., if new entry is only possible by purchasing an existing business), it becomes possible for the firms to obtain tacit agreement on prices and market areas and become free of the fear of new competition or the fear that competitors will attempt to undercut them. Management of these firms will not face the same cost-reducing imperatives as local governments do, since the competition has been limited. Furthermore, over the long run, what is left of the competitive structure under restricted entry may dissolve through mergers. Therefore, with severely restricted franchising, though efficiency may increase in the short run, in the long run the providers may be reduced to a few monopolistic firms, and management incentives to minimize costs may deteriorate, resulting in higher charges to clients.[6]

On the other hand, if many firms compete for the franchises, there will be incentives for efficiencies. There also will be special costs, such as marketing and possible inefficient spacing of routes (e.g., for solid waste collection) and fewer economies of scale, thus reducing the advantage of having a large number of service suppliers.

A happy medium is needed, one that provides enough competition to provide motivation to improve efficiency and lower prices but at the same time one that provides a large enough share of the business to individual firms so that efficient service delivery can occur.

**Choices Available to Clients.** Franchising gives customers more choice of suppliers if these suppliers are not given exclusive franchises. This permits customers to shop around for a low-cost, high-quality supplier. However, as noted, the benefits could be short-lived if suppliers become monopolistic.

**Distributional Effects.** Little direct empirical evidence exists on distributional effects (e.g., in solid waste collection, taxis, or utilities). Franchising of local government services will put more pressure on low-income families to pay for services on time or have their service terminated. What may happen with franchising, such as with solid waste collection, is that low-income families less able to pay will be less attractive as customers and in any case may try to reduce or avoid payments when they can. They may, for example, prefer to reduce their use of the service by taking their own garbage directly to landfills. This might allow low-income property owners to lower their costs but also can lead to a lowered level of service for poor neighborhoods. For example, low-income households are likely to opt for once-a-week rather than twice-a-week collection. Whether this is a socially desirable consequence is a matter of debate.

**Staying Power and Potential for Service Disruption.** Once a government goes into franchising, the process is likely to last for several years. There is additional likelihood of service disruption with private firms because of higher probabilities that the individual private firms will have financial or labor difficulties, enough to interrupt services for at least short periods of time. Franchises, as with contracts, should provide for such contingencies, with penalties for firms that are unable to deliver service within a reasonable amount of time, and with retention by government of some delivery capability (but the latter will add to government costs).

**Quality/Effectiveness of Service.** Most of the advantages and disadvantages of contracting also apply to franchising. In addition, since customers deal directly with private firms, the households will, with nonexclusive franchises, have some choice as to the level of service and be able to have some selection of suppliers, for example, those with reputations for quality service.

On the other hand, private firms are likely to be more cost conscious than quality conscious. As with contracting, if conditions approximate the free market, or if the service level and quality are regulated by the government, service levels should reach appropriate and desired levels. But to the extent that entry is closed and competition is light, franchising can lead to reduced level and quality of service.

Little empirical information is currently available on effects of different franchising arrangements on service quality and delivery, as compared to service quality and delivery under nonfranchise systems.

**Feasibility.** Proposals to change to franchising or to contracting will likely cause considerable resistance from government employee associations and unions and from some citizen groups. State laws or local ordinances may have to be changed to permit franchising. Recent suits against the use of exclusive franchises by local government (involving cable television and ground transportation to and from city airports) have raised legal questions.[7] Franchising represents a major switch in service delivery approach, and the sponsors will need to expend much effort to gain its acceptance. Even more effort will be required for franchising than for contracting, since questions will inevitably be raised by individual households and other customers about problems of control over service quality and rates. And franchising arrangements can become quite complex.

**Overall Impact.** The introduction of franchising will have a major impact. It will substantially reduce government costs by shifting the costs directly to customers. Franchising seems likely to be popular with those who believe that local governments should do as little as possible and that the private sector is much better able to provide efficient service. However, the consequences will depend on the extent to which a strong level of competition exists through reasonably open access to the franchises or the extent to which there are effective controls on service levels and charges under exclusive, single-firm franchises. Without these safeguards, the advantages of franchising are likely to deteriorate rapidly and to result in higher costs or substantially lower quality of service to the public.

# CHAPTER 4

# GRANTS AND SUBSIDIES

## Definition and Rationale

With grants and subsidies, the government makes a financial or in-kind contribution to private organizations or to individuals to encourage them to provide a service so that the government does not have to provide it. This approach may occur as part of other approaches, particularly those in which a government gives up a service but wants to encourage a private agency to take over that service.

Grants or subsidies may be one-time awards to encourage the private agency or individual to undertake an activity, or they may be annual payments, perhaps to enable the private agency to hold down charges to users, especially where the government regulates the charges or service levels. For example, in transit systems where the companies are not permitted to raise fares or remove unprofitable routes, subsidies can be used to reimburse the company. (Note that partly because of such restrictions, most private transit companies have gotten out of the business. In 1978, only 9 percent of transit passenger miles were carried by private companies.)

The rationale for this approach is that the grant or subsidy is expected to be an expensive way to encourage private activity that will benefit the community and that could not be done as inexpensively or as well by the government.

Little has been written on this particular approach as a whole, although extensive experience with it exists in specific services such as transit companies.

## Examples

Governments occasionally make grants to encourage the development and continuation of cultural programs, such as the arts, museums, and zoos. Grants occur where the local government itself does not wish to be responsible for the full activity, a more costly alternative, but feels it needs to provide supplemental funds to keep all or some portion of the activity going that otherwise would not exist.

Governments can lease public hospitals or give them to a private firm as part of an arrangement to encourage the private agency to take over the health services. If the lease is at a less-than-market rate, it can be considered a subsidy.

Another relatively common example of a subsidy is funding given to operate the community's public transit system. The government may also provide buses to the firm to help the firm get started.

Grants or subsidies to individuals are illustrated by (1) homesteading incentives in which homes owned by the local government are given to individuals if the persons rehabilitates the homes and (2) various crime-solvers' programs in which payments are made to individuals for anonymously providing information leading to the solving of major crimes.

For the most part, grants generally are to nonprofit, private agencies. Subsidies, as in the hospital example, may be to for-profit firms where it is believed to be in the public interest, particularly to avoid large costs that otherwise would be required.

## Evaluation

**Cost of Government Service.** Government costs increase by the amount of the grant or subsidy. However, since the intent is to encourage a private agency to undertake the service at an overall lower cost to the government, grants and subsidies should reduce the net cost to the government—if the government would otherwise have to provide that service. Each individual application of grants or subsidies should, of course, have its own specific cost analysis to determine the net cost impact. Administrative cost for grants probably will be low, since there is no necessity for special government activity such as day-to-day monitoring of the recipient. However, calculation of subsidies can be a major task requiring considerable effort if the size of the subsidy is linked to the profitability of a private, for-profit firm.

**Cost to Citizens.** Some grants and subsidies are provided to enable the private agency to hold down its charges to consumers (such as bus fares). In such cases, direct costs to users will go down, though nonusers will also be paying the cost through taxes used to fund the grant or subsidy.

**Choices Available to Clients.** Grants and subsidies permit added choice to the extent that they permit the continuation or introduction of an activity that otherwise would not be feasible. They do not, in general, aim at providing added competition, though grants or subsidies can be made to help another provider enter an otherwise hard-to-enter or monopolistic service area.

**Quality/Effectiveness of Service.** The grant approach has no obvious general effect on quality, except to the extent that a subsidized private agency is able to provide an improved service. There appears to be no evidence that such subsidies have led to significantly altered service quality or effectiveness, even in the operation of transit systems.

**Distributional Effects.** The use of grants and subsidies does not inherently affect the distribution of services among groups within the community. Depending on the purpose of the grant or subsidy, however, there can be direct consequences. Grants to cultural activities will primarily benefit those who participate in such cultural activities. Grants to transit systems operated by private companies will tend to benefit directly the users of the public transit system, especially to the extent that grants keep transportation costs down for users by subsidizing the operation. Subsidies to transit systems, it can be argued, also can help automobile users and others by reducing congestion and air pollution.

**Staying Power and Potential for Service Disruption.** Sometimes the purpose of grants or subsidies is to prevent a service disruption, such as by providing funds to an organization that otherwise would go out of business. On the other hand, if the subsidy is to a private agency to encourage it to take over a public activity, there is a somewhat greater risk that the private agency, as compared with a public agency, would have a major service disruption caused by a financial problem, bankruptcy, or strike.

If the recipient private agency is dependent on annual subsidies or grants, this could become a problem. The local government is likely to review the size of the subsidy annually. When funds become scarce, pressure will increase to reduce or eliminate the subsidy.

**Feasibility.** Depending on the specific application, there could be legal constraints and also resistance by groups in the community that do not receive the grants or subsidies. The relative lack of precedent of this approach may make local legislatures reluctant to try the grant or subsidy approach.

**Overall Impact.** Grants and subsidies can be quite important in altering service delivery by encouraging a private agency to take over a major government activity, such as a public hospital or a transit operation. Applications of grants and subsidies to transit systems have not worked; in fact, many private transit companies for a number of reasons have been taken over by public bodies.

# CHAPTER 5

# VOUCHERS

## Definitions and Rationale

The government provides vouchers to citizens needing the service. The citizens are then free to choose the organization from which to buy the goods or services, using the vouchers. The organization returns the vouchers to the government for payment. The vouchers can be used only for the specified goods or services. The organization that provides the service can be public or private. The local government can set limitations as to which organizations are eligible to receive the vouchers. Unlike the use of franchises, payments for the service, at least up to the level provided by the voucher, are made by the government. Unlike subsidies and grants, vouchers are given by the government to the consumer and not to the producer.

The rationale for vouchers is that they give clients increased choice of suppliers. To the extent that there is not a highly constrained set of eligible suppliers, clients should be better able to obtain the type of service they want. Suppliers deficient in quality or level of service presumably would not be used.

The voucher approach is usually not aimed at reducing the costs of the service. Some advocates, however, believe that the added competition among suppliers will lower the costs.[1] How the actual cash value of the voucher is determined in specific application is a key factor. If vouchers are set at recent average costs, savings will tend to be small. If their value is set at levels of the most efficient suppliers, savings could be substantial.[2]

Vouchers are applicable to services that are primarily provided to individuals, services such as those listed in the columns to the right of *Service* in exhibit 4.

## Examples

There are few actual examples of local government using vouchers. The most well-known example has been the use of vouchers in the Alum Rock School District of San Jose, California, as part of a demonstration supported by the National Institute of Education in the early 1970s. The demonstration terminated in midcourse.[3] Only public schools were involved and only some schools in the district participated. Parents could choose the schools their children would attend, and the schools received credit for each child, equal to the amount of money expended by the district in the most recent fiscal year divided by total enrollment.

The educational voucher system required major new administrative support services, special budgeting, and more careful school attendance accounting. The evaluation at the end of the first year of the demonstration (before it was terminated but too soon to come to definitive conclusions) was ambiguous on student test outcomes. Schools experienced substantial funding uncertainties and major problems arose in developing the details of the voucher system. The trial showed a small positive increase both in parent satisfaction and in attitudes toward school governance. Parents using vouchers became more in favor of parent involvement in school and in a variety of school decisions.

Michigan citizens, in November 1978, defeated an initiative that would have removed schools from property tax support and would have set up a statewide voucher system, but there appears not to have been much marketing or specific information on the proposal to citizens. A new proposal for testing vouchers was attempted in California in 1982.[4] The proposal, however, did not gain enough signatures to appear on the 1982 California ballot.

Vouchers for housing for the poor have been the other major application. The federal government sponsored an experiment from 1973 to 1979 in twelve metropolitan areas, involving 15,000 families and $160 million. The objective was to improve housing conditions for low-income people without building subsidized housing for them. Analysis found some successes in the experiment, especially its ability to reach the poor and reduce the share of family income going for rent, without increasing housing prices. But the experiment did not improve housing quality appreciably nor did it stimulate an increase in the amount of housing investment. And less than one-half of the eligible population participated in the voluntary program. A major effort went into designing, administering, and evaluating the experiment, including $83 million in research funds.[5] The complexity and magnitude of this effort make its relevance to local governments quite uncertain.

There have been proposals to use vouchers to permit clients to choose the providers for certain social services, including day care, homemaker services, and mental health placement services such as foster homes or group homes.[6] Hennepin County, Minnesota, began in 1982 a voucher system for day care for income-eligible families. The program has increased greatly the number of day care facilities that eligible families can use—from nineteen centers located in two areas of the county to several hundred centers spread across the county. Because many of the added facilities provide lower-cost care, the county anticipates lower per-day care costs under the voucher system.

Vouchers are also being tried for transportation for the elderly and the handicapped in San Leandro, California (64,000 population), and Kinston, North Carolina (25,000). Clients pay a small fee for coupons worth considerably more. These can be used for local paratransit such as taxis. The coupons are usually provided for citizens who cannot use buses.

## Evaluation

**Cost of Government Service.** Little information is available to date on the use of vouchers for local services. As noted earlier, reducing cost does not appear to be a major objective for voucher systems. The educational voucher system did not show a significant cost reduction after one year, but that was a highly specialized case and can hardly be accepted as representative of other local government services. Proponents of vouchers believe that their use would increase competition among numerous providers instead of relying on municipal monopolies, and that this should result in lower costs. A key uncertainty is whether provider agencies, especially if private, would be better able to lobby for price increases than the government agency, thus increasing costs.

Clearly, significant administrative costs are involved—for providing the vouchers and overseeing that they are handled properly and that payment claims are processed correctly.

Since the vouchers would substitute for government service, the net cost to the government would depend on its savings in government delivery versus the costs of the vouchers. It seems likely that costs would be roughly the same, and probably even higher, at least initially, because of the administrative costs.

**Cost to Citizens.** Since the voucher is merely substituting for government direct service, and assuming that the service would be about the same, the cost to citizens should be nearly equivalent to that of municipal delivery.

**Choices Available to Clients.** This is the big advantage of vouchers. Recipients of the vouchers would be able to select the supplier, presumably choosing ones that provide the kinds and amounts of services they want, and doing without those service elements that they do not want or can do without.

**Quality/Effectiveness of Service.** To the extent that the added choice enables clients to better match their wants with what they actually receive, the resulting quality and level of service should be more appropriate. This result will depend upon the extent to which citizens are able to obtain information on the quality of providers and thus make informed choices. If such information is lacking and if the private providers put their emphasis on cost rather than quality, it is quite conceivable that quality would diminish.

**Distributional Effects.** Generalizations cannot be made about distributional effects without looking at the specific application. Some applications could be for disadvantaged clients (e.g., for social services) who might particularly benefit.

**Staying Power and Potential for Service Disruption.** Because of the potential for difficulties and mishandling of vouchers, this approach seems likely to continue to be controversial and to face frequent attack from various groups within the community.

Since private providers are more subject to labor and financial problems than government is, there are more likely to be short-term disruptions and problems of continuity. The clients may experience difficulties before being able to find another provider.

**Feasibility.** Changing over to a voucher system requires substantial governmental effort to sell such an operation with all its many complications. As indicated in the California education voucher experiment, there are likely to be many initial problems in administration. Misuse of the vouchers is a potential problem; special care is needed to avoid abuses associated with handling money.

**Overall Impact.** Given the highly limited experience with voucher systems in local government, this approach should be considered highly experimental. Major cost savings to the government are not likely. The big advantage, clearly, is the additional choice vouchers provide to clients. Vouchers should be used where the client can be expected to have sufficient information to make informed choices. Voucher systems seem wise for some human services such as day care, but pilot experiments are required before one could make a reasonable appraisal as to their usefulness. Vouchers might best be tried initially in those situations where the government already is providing funds to nongovernmental agencies, such as social services for low-income families, and, thus, the proposal would face less resistance from public employees.

# CHAPTER 6

# VOLUNTEERS

## Definition and Rationale

With the volunteer approach, individuals in the jurisdiction provide free help to a government agency, thereby reducing the amount of government activity that otherwise would be required. Volunteers may supplement government services (e.g., volunteer library aides) or wholly provide a service (for example, fire departments with stations staffed completely by volunteers). In this report, the approach is limited to volunteers who work directly for a local government; it does not include individuals doing volunteer work for a private (such as a charitable) organization or doing work primarily to help themselves. (The latter arrangement is discussed in this chapter under "Self-help".)

The use of volunteers for local activities such as recreation and library aides and other social service activities is not new. What is different, however, is the current interest in more systematic efforts by governments to identify jobs for volunteers within many local government agencies, to recruit the volunteers for those jobs, and to provide guidelines, technical assistance, training, and administration for the volunteer activity within the whole government. Most volunteer activity in local governments is still specific to individual city departments. Only relatively recently have broad-coverage volunteer efforts started—in such local governments as Virginia Beach (population 260,000), New Orleans (560,000), San Leandro, California (64,000), and Los Angeles (3,000,000). The state of Virginia in 1977 passed a Virginia State Government Volunteers Act, which encourages use of volunteers in state agencies and established a Division of Volunteerism to provide assistance to local and state agencies.

The primary attraction of volunteers is that they are free. They are usually used to undertake tasks that otherwise would not get done. In most cases, local governments' official policy is that volunteers are not intended to replace paid employees but to do activities that otherwise could not be supported. In periods of very tight funding, however, governments may be tempted to lay off personnel where there is a reasonable chance of substituting volunteer help.

What are the needed conditions for successful use of volunteers? The city of Virginia Beach identified the following prerequisites for using volunteers successfully:[1]

- Departmental tasks can be effectively accomplished by volunteers
- The city has an adequate and qualified pool of volunteer resources
- Departments are willing to use volunteers
- City departments are able to recruit and to train volunteers

A key question is whether sufficient volunteers exist in the community. The 1981 Gallup Poll Survey on Volunteering (commissioned by Independent Sector) indicated that over half the adults and teenagers reported some form of organized volunteer activity in 1980. Much of the volunteering, however, focused on religious activity and education (such as PTA) and was done for the private nonprofit sector rather than for governments.[2]

Governments with volunteer programs, particularly those centrally coordinated, often tally the number of volunteers and hours worked. The communities may then apply a dollar value to the work based on assumed equivalent salary rates for various age and occupational groups. Virginia Beach, for example, in the third quarter of calendar year 1981 reported a total of 1,776 volunteers putting in 53,343 hours (an average of 30 hours each) for a total value of $351,839 (an average of $6.60 per hour). This was equivalent to approximately twenty-six staff years for a single quarter. Approximately twelve city agencies were included. Forty percent of these volunteer hours was for the parks and recreation department.

Volunteer use is likely to be most applicable where the needed job skills can be developed quickly or where many citizens are likely to enjoy the activity,—for example, library, recreation, and fire programs. Volunteer fire fighters require extensive special training, but many persons are sufficiently intrigued by the job to dedicate many hours to it.

There are a number of potential problems with the use of volunteers:

- Their availability may be limited to brief periods of time and perhaps unusual times, such as evenings and weekends. The Virginia Beach example given earlier indicated an average of 30 hours per volunteer for the quarter—about three-quarters of a work week. (Virginia Beach obtained a relatively high proportion of its volunteers from its older population, which had a volunteer rate 43 percent higher than expected based on its proportion in the population. The elderly still made up only 10 percent of all volunteers.)

- Dependability of volunteers is not always certain, since there is less motivation to appear on schedule. Some governments are trying to treat volunteers as if they were members of the work force, requiring strict attendance. This requirement is difficult to enforce.

- High turnover of volunteers means that retraining programs are needed frequently. "Volunteer involvement can be rather unpredictable."[3]

- Volunteers require supervision and administrative effort.

- If the volunteer program is not handled well, friction may develop between staff and volunteers and staff morale may decline. If volunteers become substitutes for city staff, this could cause a difficult problem.

Time and financial costs are associated with operating a comprehensive volunteer program. Central coordination may be necessary, though part of this probably can be volunteer effort. Individual managers need to make the effort to identify jobs and write job descriptions for volunteers, and to use publicity to find the necessary volunteers. Subsequently, a need exists to keep track of the hours spent and to document the amount and type of volunteer activity.

## Evaluation

**Cost of Government Service.** The use of volunteers should reduce costs somewhat, if volunteers are not used solely to provide extra levels of service but also perform activities that government employees would otherwise undertake. There are administrative costs to using volunteers, including advertising for volunteers, training, special supervision, and keeping track of the volunteers. There may also be payments for liability insurance and even pension payments such as for volunteer fire fighters. We have not found any analyses that estimate administrative costs or the net cost savings to individual agencies and the government as a whole. However, cities with governmentwide programs usually attempt to calculate a dollar value for volunteers' time. Because of the usual limitation on the use of volunteers to provide extra service rather than to replace government employees, volunteer time cannot be claimed as actual cost savings. As local governments are forced to cut back funding levels, this policy may change. The use of volunteers, as currently applied in local governments, does not have a major effect on government costs. One exception has been in the use of volunteer fire fighters (such as in Montgomery County, Maryland). But whether the fire fighting experience can be transferred to other agencies is not at all clear. The most likely prospects are all-volunteer or mainly volunteer libraries, with the government continuing to pay facility maintenance and material costs. Recreation agencies are the next most likely candidates to become heavily reliant on volunteers.

**Cost to Citizens.** Other than any added costs to the volunteers themselves, there do not appear to be significant cost consequences for citizens. Presumably, the use of volunteers should reduce taxes or fees and charges for the service provided, and this clearly appears to be the case in fire departments with heavy use of volunteers. A 1966 study[4] concluded that a combination, part-paid, part-volunteer department (such as in Montgomery County, Maryland, where the study was done) offers fire protection equivalent to that of paid departments, and at a lower cost. The report further stated that a combination department offers significantly better protection than an all-volunteer fire department.

**Choices Available to Clients.** To the extent that the use of volunteers permits the government to offer extra programs or extra hours of service, this gives more choice to citizens. However, this approach is not aimed at providing greater choice.

**Quality/Effectiveness of Service.** Little information is available, other than the above-mentioned study on the Montgomery County Fire Department. If high-caliber volunteers are available, the service quality could increase. If volunteers are not wisely chosen, trained, and fitted to their tasks, service quality could suffer.

**Distributional Effects.** The use of volunteers does not seem to have significant, or controversial, distributional effects.

**Staying Power and Potential for Service Disruption.** A government will have to maintain continuous effort to recruit replacement volunteers. It is unlikely that volunteers can be depended on for long periods of time, such as even one year. Because of lower dependability, some minor service disruption seems likely to occur periodically.

**Feasibility.** Major obstacles to the establishment of small-scale volunteer programs, whether they are citywide or department programs, do not appear to exist. The major feasibility question is the availability of volunteers in the community. A small volunteer program is quite feasible in most communities. Large-scale use of volunteers, however, has two major problems: (1) sufficient volunteers may not be available and (2) employee organizations are likely to battle if they perceive that the jobs of paid employees are being threatened.

**Overall Impact.** Small-scale increases in service levels and minor reductions in service costs seem likely with volunteer programs. Almost no evidence exists that use of volunteers, in other than fire control, has been extensive enough, thus far, to permit major cost reduction. Large-scale programs with substantial impacts seem unlikely. However, part-volunteer fire departments, which already exist, and possibly heavily volunteer libraries and recreation programs could become more widespread in communities with major fiscal constraints.

Information on the cost per unit of output of volunteers, plus information on the quality of that output, is needed to provide a better perspective on the economic and service effects of volunteer programs.

# CHAPTER 7

# SELF-HELP

## Definition and Rationale

In self-help, the government encourages individuals or groups, such as neighborhood associations, to undertake activities for their own benefit. Although there is a similarity between self-help and other alternatives such as voluntarism and the encouragement of private organizations to take over an activity, the key element in self-help is that individuals or groups are encouraged to undertake an activity in which the primary client group is themselves. In this report, indigenous groups that provide help to others in their neighborhoods (such as churches and Alcoholics Anonymous), are included under "Encouragement of Private Organizations to Take Over an Activity."

In self-help the emphasis rests on finding solutions to one's own problems and developing self-reliance. With self-help groups, mutual assistance and community action are also prominent themes. The assumption is that citizens, at least under certain conditions, will be willing to help themselves and will be better able than the government to provide the proper level and type of service. Advocates generally believe that the individual or group can provide the required service at less cost than the government can.[1]

Two major problems arise: (1) the possible lack of incentive to individuals or groups to undertake the activity and (2) the "free-rider" problem, that is, if only some of a group undertake self-help, others who have not participated in the effort will share in the benefits. Thus, self-help efforts may require special actions such as specific legal agreements among the affected households or special regulatory and tax changes to encourage the activity.

## Examples

Examples of self-help focusing on individuals include government publicity to encourage exercise or other personal physical and mental health care activities (thereby avoiding potential public health costs), encouragement of car-pool programs (reducing congestion and various transportation costs), and encouraging households or businesses to install fire alarms and sprinkler systems (and thereby reduce future fire control costs).[2] Another classic example is switching from back-door to curbside solid waste collection. In most instances where this has been done, however, it has been a unilateral move by the government to cut costs and is more an example of "reducing the level of service" than a self-help option. If, however, the citizens volunteer, it probably can be labeled self-help. Similarly, a government might have citizens carry their solid waste to a landfill or incinerator, replacing government pickup. This option is more appropriate for smaller and more rural communities.

Some other potential applications include having households in a neighborhood take care of street and sidewalk sweeping, or even temporary maintenance of the roads or curbs in front of their own homes. As noted under "Franchises," in St. Paul citizens can take out a permit from the city to replace curbs. The city has licensed a number of companies to do the curb replacements. The citizens can contract for the work or replace the curbs themselves.[3]

Group self-help activity is more common than individual activities. An example is neighborhood watch groups. Many of these have formed throughout the country since the National Sheriffs' Association gave them a push in 1976. Typically, citizens patrol their areas. They are usually unarmed and act as auxiliary eyes and ears for the police, noting suspicious activity and reporting it via citizens band radio or telephone. Local police departments may provide training on laws concerning citizen's arrest and on how to be an effective witness.

New York City in its 1980 Urban Park and Recovery Plan proposed that citizen community groups take responsibility for the security and maintenance of some neighborhood parks. If the groups agreed, the city would then rehabilitate the park. For example, soccer teams would sign agreements to take care of the routine maintenance of part of a park. Local block associations could establish citizen patrols to assure personal security and reduce vandalism.[4]

A proposed, more extreme, version of self-help is to permit neighborhood associations in urban areas to deliver a wide range of services, including refuse collection, street and sidewalk maintenance, street patrol, street lighting, caring for nearby recreation facilities, and day care centers.[5] Capital-intensive services, however, such as water and sewer services, do not lend themselves well to such neighborhood association control.

The incentive for the association would be property tax relief or service fee reduction. Thus, this example represents a combination of self-help and the use of tax policy. The tax reduction would be related to the actual cost of the service and presumably would save the local government that amount. In another variation, the government might actually contract with the association for the services.

To avoid the free-rider problem, the tax credit would be made available only if *all* property owners in the neighborhood agreed to attach provisions to deeds establishing automatic membership in the neighborhood association (not unlike homeowners' associations in condominiums and other high-density housing areas). The association would then be free to establish whatever service arrangements best met members' needs. They could provide the service themselves or contract for those services. Such an arrangement would leave the choice of services and service levels up to the members of the association and therefore presumably would be more responsive to the needs and wants of the membership.

In St. Louis and adjoining University City, some residents own their streets and have set up nonprofit corporations. There are currently over 1,000 private streets, each owned by a private association empowered through legal agreements with all property owners to levy assessments to pay for maintenance and improvements. The cities continue to provide police, fire, and utility services. St. Louis gives the households on these streets a property tax abatement in lieu of not having to do street maintenance. Researchers found that private-street residents had a greater sense of community stability and security, and that crime rates were lower. The researchers, however, also pointed out that the financial burden could become substantial for moderate-income families having to pay yearly assessments, occasional special assessments for major repairs, and an initial requirement to share the cost of purchasing the underground service lines from the city.[6]

## Evaluation

**Cost of Government Service.** Since citizen activity is substituted for government activity, government cost should be reduced.

Some government cost will be necessary to work out the self-help arrangement, whether it is for publicity to encourage the individual toward the activity or for arrangements with neighborhood associations. The latter could involve considerable time by government employees, since it will probably be necessary to work individually with each neighborhood and to work out any offsetting tax or service fee reductions.

A potential problem with self-help generated by neighborhood associations is that for some services, some areas of the community may choose the self-help, but others will not, leading to a geographic crazy quilt. Government costs to service the remaining areas could increase. For example, service street sweeping or refuse collection crews would have more downtime while traveling between areas of the community, and crews might be confused as to where they are to work. With each neighborhood group undertaking particular activities in its own neighborhood, the question arises as to whether this is the most efficient way to do the work. For some activities, economies of scale and the use of professional specialists could be lost through this greater decentralization of service delivery.

Governments will need to monitor the work done by groups to ascertain whether what is done meets minimum quality levels for activities such as curb repair or park maintenance. However, some forms of self-help will probably require only a small amount of local government monitoring. Added cost and effort will be needed by the government to determine the amount of the appropriate reduction in charges or taxes for individual households and then to administer these. Little empirical information on actual cost savings or administrative costs exists at the present time.

**Cost to Citizens.** To the extent that self-help reduces taxes or fees and charges that citizens would otherwise have had to pay the government, citizen costs are reduced by self-help. Note, however, in some forms of self-help, groups themselves contract out for services, so cost savings may not be large (and conceivably costs could be higher because of the lower volume of the service purchased by any one group). Finally, whereas local taxes are deductible for federal income taxes, any payments made by groups or individuals for contracted services probably would not be.

**Choices Available to Clients.** This option gives citizens more flexibility in how and to what degree the activity is done. It can also be argued, however, that self-help may give some citizens more responsibility than they want, for example, by requiring members of neighborhood associations to participate and then having either to spend time debating those choices or giving up their added choice. Will control shift to a relatively few who dominate the neighborhood?

**Quality/Effectiveness of Service.** On the one hand, it can be argued that when people do things for themselves, the activity is more likely to be at the needed quality, at least the quality that they themselves feel they need. On the other hand, to the extent that self-help is done by part-time amateurs rather than professionals, problems can arise. A local park could be in better condition if the group responsible takes special care and effort, but it could be in worse condition if group members have difficulty finding time to get the work done properly, if they do not like the work, or if they do not have the proper equipment or talent to do the work. Greater self-esteem and greater community spirit and morale can be important benefits of self-help programs. Unfortunately, little empirical evidence is currently available on the arrangements and conditions under which beneficial or negative effects result.

In one particular application, that of neighborhood watch programs, some limited evidence exists. Denver reported robberies down about one-third in neighborhood watch areas. The New Orleans burglary rate was reduced by 10 percent, a reduction some officials attributed to its 200 neighborhood watch units. For the first nine months in 1981, serious crimes of violence decreased in Los Angeles within locations of extensive new citizen patrol activity.[7] An evaluation completed in 1977 of Spokane's program found no significant difference in the burglary rate or the rate of no-force burglaries during the first year after the program was introduced.[8] A nationwide mail survey, however, found three times as many police departments reported decreases in the rate of burglary than reported increases after the program was introduced. About 90 percent of the responding police departments reported improved police-public relations.[9] The director of security for St. Paul, indicated that neighborhood watch organizations and related self-help strategies such as locking doors and neighbors looking out for one another are the best ways to deter crime.[10] An evaluation of the Law Enforcement Assisstance Administration (LEAA)-sponsored National Neighborhood Watch program described the effort in Monroe County, New York (population 700,000), as highly successful in reducing residential burglaries.[11]

With self-help, community participants are presumably better able to identify their own needs, and this should lead to a better match of services and needs.

**Distributional Effects.** Some persons or some neighborhoods will be better able to provide self-help than others. For example, some neighborhoods may be financially unable to replace their curbs, and the result of self-help in those neighborhoods would be curbs in poorer condition than curbs in other parts of the community. To the extent, however, that this represents individual choice and permits households to save money, this is an advantage.

A major potential problem with permitting neighborhood associations to take over basic service delivery is the possibility that rich neighborhoods would secede, leaving less affluent neighborhoods with what could be higher costs and higher taxes because of increased unit cost to the government.

**Staying Power and Potential for Service Disruption.** Since self-help depends on voluntary participation of the individual, it is possible that public enthusiasm for the activity, or the citizens' time available to perform it, could decline, with the result that the local government would once again have to take over the service. There is little evidence, other than the St. Louis private streets example, as to whether self-help activities remain in existence for prolonged periods of time. An examination of neighborhood watch activities, many of which were introduced in the mid-1970s, would shed light on this question. The lack of an institutional structure can weaken the lasting quality of self-help programs. The proposed use of formal deed stipulations, discussed earlier, would provide a more formal and probably longer-lasting arrangement.

**Feasibility.** Where self-help is to be provided by neighborhood groups, government effort to put the activity together is needed, perhaps in several locations within the jurisdiction. To the extent that the groups themselves generate self-help, government activity will be minor. But if the government wants to encourage and start such activity, its effort could be major and only partly successful.

A major feasibility issue arises where reductions to fees and charges, and especially to property taxes, are involved. Changes in state as well as local legislation may be prerequisites.

**Overall Impact.** Self-help is an attractive concept. It seems likely to reduce the cost of government. Applications not accompanied by other forms of incentives, such as regulatory or tax reduction incentives, however, appear quite limited in their potential for offering major cost reduction opportunities. Unfortunately, use of such incentives can require major legislative changes and considerable effort to achieve fair tax offsets. For such applications as neighborhood watch programs, in fact, it is probable that little immediate cost savings are accomplished. The size of police departments remains the same, at least initially. Should, however, such self-help programs remain in place for a period of time, and significantly reduce the amount of crime, then police departments might be reduced.

# CHAPTER 8

# USE OF REGULATORY AND TAXING AUTHORITY

## Definition and Rationale

In this approach, governments use regulatory and taxing authority to encourage the private sector (organizations or individuals) to provide public services or at least to reduce the need for public services.[1]

Regulation and taxation are complicated topics. In one form or another local governments have used them for years, particularly for controlling housing and commercial activities. Regulatory and taxing authority can be used to affect costs to private sector individuals and businesses and the way they do business. Regulation applies to both profit and nonprofit agencies, but taxation applies primarily to for-profit organizations. Both can be used to affect the behavior of individuals and households. The use of taxing authority is similar to the use of grants or subsidies; in fact, tax reduction measures can be considered a form of subsidy.

The intent is to reshape local regulations and taxes to promote and partly reflect certain market activities and to encourage the desired behavior by the private sector. This approach can thus be used to encourage private sector activity to meet community social needs. Reducing regulations can remove barriers to entry of alternative providers (profit or nonprofit) and reduce the costs to private sector organizations. Note, however, that often local governments may have only limited authority. For many services, such as social services, the most significant regulations are imposed by federal or state governments.

Regulation and taxing modifications are often used in combination with other approaches, such as encouraging neighborhood associations to undertake self-help.

## Examples

**Regulation/Deregulation.** The primary example of local regulation is the application of various land use controls such as zoning. This report focuses on services other than housing and economic development and thus will not examine this application.

Local governments can undertake deregulation to reduce licensing requirements for various types of human service care providers, or to permit more transportation providers to enter the market. For example, requirements for specific types and amounts of training of caseworkers can be reduced to permit alternative types of care programs, such as street-front walk-in centers. Eligibility regulations for potential adoptive parents can be reduced to encourage more persons to adopt and to reduce delays in placements. Unfortunately, many of these requirements may come from the state or federal government and therefore may not be directly controllable by a local government. A similar example is the introduction of various inspection and code requirements, such as fire and safety requirements. If overly stringent, these requirements discourage certain providers, such as providers of day care and residential facilities. Clearly, there is a balance between protecting clients from hazards and overly protecting them from hazards that may be quite small but relatively costly to eliminate.

For public transportation, regulations concerning taxicab operators, private commuter bus lines, and other types of paratransit operators greatly affect competition and the options open to the public. Transportation authorities have often resisted opening up their monopolies to other companies or other types of transportation. To some extent, this is necessary to avoid having to share profitable routes that enable the company with a monopoly to subsidize unprofitable routes and service. The Indianapolis Bell Cab Company, however, introduced fifteen-passenger jitney express vans, despite opposition by the transit authority. In Chicago, a charter and subscription bus service is being formed by commuter groups.

A World Bank study of Bangkok, Istanbul, and Calcutta reported that private minibuses permitted the cities to avoid an extra 40 percent more buses for peak periods. The study found that most companies charged the same as the city buses and made a profit, while the city buses covered only 70 percent of their costs.[2]

Deregulation of the number of taxis and their fares is sometimes proposed. In 1979, the city of Los Angeles removed the limit on the number of cabs but retained fare controls (as has the District of Columbia, Atlanta, and Honolulu). The city of San Diego lifted its limits on both the number of cabs and fares (except for a high cap) but required cabs to post fares in their windows. The costs in October 1980 were $1.00–$1.20 per mile, below the $1.50 cap. Both Seattle, Washington, and Eugene, Oregon, abolished fare controls in 1978. Increased use of cabs and their coverage of more locations, not just high-volume runs, has been claimed for these deregulations.[3]

Regulations of fares and routes can force public or private companies to operate on unprofitable routes and at fares below their actual cost. This probably has driven many companies out of the public transit business. There are reasons for such regulation, especially to provide low-income bus riders with reasonably low-cost transportation and to provide minimum levels of transportation services in relatively low traffic areas. However, particularly in the latter case, other alternatives exist; paying subsidies to deregulated paratransit companies may, for example, be less expensive than having the government supply the service.

Added regulation can be used in some instances to encourage a greater private sector role. For example, a New York City ordinance requires citizens to pick up behind their dogs, with fines for failure to do so (but, a personal observation, not many do). Regulations can be introduced that would require the use of fire alarms and sprinklers in private homes and businesses (on the assumption that this would lead to lower fire control costs, as well as fewer casualties and less property damage). An unusual form of regulation is to require dissemination of information to the public on hospital or other health provider rates and thereby encourage lower health care costs.[4]

**Taxing Authority.** Local governments have often used tax breaks for the purpose of attracting new business into a community. Tax abatements have also been used to permit older persons to remain in their homes when taxes rise to levels beyond their income. Tax reductions can be used to provide credits to homeowners, individuals, or agencies that provide certain services—for example, tax credits to homeowners who use their homes to provide day care for nonfamily members.

Tax breaks can be provided to individual homeowners or to neighborhood associations that care for their own property, such as local maintenance of streets (as discussed under "Self-help"). In Hartford, Connecticut, property tax breaks have been used for persons providing volunteer help to the city. Tax credits could be given for self-protected buildings (easing police and fire costs) or to stimulate storm-water-runoff control by homeowners, especially in locations with combined storm and sanitary sewers (thus reducing wastewater distribution and treatment costs).

## Evaluation

**Cost of Government Service.** One purpose of the use of regulatory (usually deregulation) or taxing authority is to encourage citizens to undertake activities that would reduce the cost of government services, such as encouraging more competition among private agencies or reducing the number of frills required by the government. Each particular application will vary considerably as to its implications, so it is difficult to generalize. The use of taxing authority usually involves reductions in taxes, thus reducing revenues to the government. These will offset cost savings.

Also, in many instances, local governments use these approaches more to provide additional service, and thus possibly to avoid some future government costs, rather than to reduce current costs.

Where added regulations (such as in requiring smoke detectors) or special tax reductions are used, there is likely to be significant added government administrative costs to monitor adherence.

**Cost to Citizens.** In many instances, the purpose of deregulation and special tax reduction is to permit and encourage more private agencies to participate in the delivery of service. This should reduce costs to citizens by providing them less costly options, such as a greater variety of transit modes at certain times of the day or more day care options.

**Choices Available to Clients.** Encouraging more private agencies to enter the market potentially provides more choices, for example, day care or transportation options.

**Quality/Effectiveness of Service.** This can be a controversial issue. Regulatory and tax reduction efforts are not usually directed at improving the quality of services except to the extent that the citizen will have more choice. Of particular concern is the fact that regulations proposed for deregulation, when first introduced, often were intended to protect the public, such as staffing and facility requirements for human service programs. If these regulations are relaxed as part of a deregulatory effort, will there be a reduction in the protection originally sought? Proponents of deregulation argue that many such requirements, such as those for specially trained and educated human service workers, add little to service quality. For example, highly trained personnel may not be as effective as lesser trained but more indigenous workers who are likely to be able to give more personal care. Little empirical evidence exists based on systematic experimentation, but some researchers have identified case studies suggesting that indigenous workers have accomplished much more in human services, for example, in helping problem juveniles.[5]

**Distributional Effects.** Effects can be quite complex. One thing is clear: the use of regulatory and taxing authority is likely to alter the distribution of costs and benefits among citizens. Certain deregulations, such as removing constraints to permit new firms to come into the market, whether relating to institutional care, day care, or paratransit, seem likely to help lower-income families. However, it can also be argued that taking away these regulations could increase hazards for these groups who are major clients for these services. For example, the augmentation of paratransit could provide more opportunities for those in the suburbs but could weaken the city transit company, forcing it to increase its rates, possibly hurting central-city clients. However, promulgators of such deregulation usually believe that the opposite would happen. The easy answer here is that "it depends."

**Staying Power and Potential for Service Disruption.** Since the use of regulatory and taxing authority is controlled by the government, the actions potentially can be permanent. However, they also can be reversed should negative consequences occur. This itself is probably a good thing. The pull and tug of political power, however, can bring down previously undertaken deregulation and taxing decisions in spite of, or in disregard of, the overall beneficial consequences.

**Feasibility.** Regulatory and taxing actions can be highly political and quite volatile. Strong opposition and major battles on most such proposals are likely. Several years may pass before proposals can be sold and implemented. Certain proposals such as deregulation of the transit business could meet considerable opposition from both public transit management and public (or private) labor organizations, as has occurred in the past.

**Overall Impact.** The use of regulatory and taxing authority is an important aspect of local governments' power. Considerable turmoil, political debate, and argument are likely. Often the stakes will be significant. Large numbers of citizens and numerous firms can be affected. Large amounts of dollars, both public and private, can be involved. If those decisions turn out to be wise ones, considerable cost savings and increased opportunities can result to both the government and the citizens. If decisions turn out to be bad, they could result in major disruptions to services and possibly increased health and safety hazards.

What is clear is that each application of regulatory or taxing authority needs to be analyzed individually and thoroughly. It is particularly important in using these applications that careful cost-benefit and cost-effectiveness analysis be undertaken, including consideration of distributional consequences, before moving ahead. This will by no means resolve the uncertainties, but it is important to obtain at least a rough grasp of the potential consequences. Such analysis can also help the government market the resulting decision to the persons affected and to the general public.

# CHAPTER 9

# ENCOURAGEMENT OF PRIVATE ORGANIZATIONS TO TAKE OVER AN ACTIVITY

## Definition and Rationale

Here the government seeks to give up responsibility for an activity but works with a private agency (profit or nonprofit) that is willing to take over the activity. This option differs from self-help in that the private agency is not comprised of those who actually are being helped (though *past* clients may be used to help new clients, as in private nonprofit drug rehabilitation programs). This approach might also involve a one-time grant or subsidy (such as giving a public hospital facility to a private firm) or tax credits. The terms *exit* and *service-shedding* have been suggested to refer to this approach.[1] This differs from situations in which the government gives up a service but still retains some major role in it, as with franchising, which was discussed earlier.[2]

The rationale is usually that the service is an inappropriate one for government and can be done more efficiently (at lower cost) or more effectively (with more personal attention and better understanding of clients' needs) by the private sector. The motivating factor in most recent exits by local governments, whether to a for-profit or nonprofit agency, has been to reduce government expenditures.

There are two important variations: (1) the new producer is a nonprofit agency and (2) the new producer is a profit-making agency.

Private nonprofit agencies providing human services are not new. Numerous private nonprofit agencies have provided services for decades, and they are indeed an alternative to government delivery. Organizations such as Alcoholics Anonymous, various drug abuse treatment programs, and a variety of church programs have been in existence for many years. Such agencies often try to avoid government funding, especially to avoid government regulations and bureaucratic requirements.

The hypothesis with nonprofit agencies is that they can provide more understanding and more personal and appropriate help than governments, and clients tend to trust them more than they would government. Government employees tend to provide more impersonal help, are more handicapped by bureaucratic regulations, and may be overburdened by large caseloads.

The term *mediating structures* has been applied to the more indigenous groups such as the family, neighborhood groups, churches, and voluntary associations.[3] Proponents would like to return to principles of past times when family members and these other groups had the major responsibility for care of their members with problems such as aging, alcohol, drugs, and other disabilities.

In the mediating structure approach, the government should strive to strengthen the family, the neighborhood, and other indigenous ties, that is, to build neighborhood capacity.[4] Such approaches seem particularly applicable for human services, including services to juveniles and the aged, mental health services, and even income-maintenance activities.

An important issue for the mediating structure approach is just how far such activites can go. In the past, dependence on the private nonprofit sector shifted to government provision when it appeared that the private charitable sector was not able to provide enough resources. In areas with large populations and more impersonal lifestyles, particularly in urban areas such as the Greater Washington, D.C., area where there are many transients, it can be especially difficult to build up the spirit of mutual help and welfare.

Also, citizens may actually prefer state or local government assistance in some instances. A 1980 Arizona State University telephone survey of 673 households in Arizona found that respondents gave "a ringing endorsement of state and local government aid for families who need *outside* help." An average of 39 percent of the respondents expressed preference for state and local government aid over four other institutions: community organizations, the federal government, churches, and private businesses. This was a figure nearly twice as high as the next preferred institution: community organizations.[5] State and local governments were preferred in thirty-one of forty-one areas, which included such concerns as "child abuse and neglect," "needs of handicapped persons," and "needs of children whose natural parents cannot care for them."

In the past, efforts to bring the private nonprofit sector into a service area have usually been initiated independently of any government participation. For public officials, the question is what can they do to encourage such activity where it appears warranted. This question has been infrequently addressed in the literature.

Suggestions that have been made include the following:[6]

- Remove financial incentives to take children (or adults) from their natural homes and place them in institutional settings

- When it is necessary to remove children (or adults) from their homes, place them when possible within the neighborhood or community and culture from which they come

- Review placement criteria so as to encourage placements with individuals or groups within the community from which the person comes

- In general, strengthen the capacity of economic institutions within neighborhoods, including individual firms

With private for-profit firms the rationale is different. The primary rationale with for-profit groups is that the private sector, being motivated by profit-making goals and facing competition, will be considerably more efficient at service delivery than government agencies will be. Therefore, government should stay out of any activity that can be done better, or just as well, by the private sector.

There can be competition in some cases between for-profit and nonprofit agencies. For example, for-profit firms have begun to enter a number of human services, such as vocational rehabilitation and homes for the elderly. In such cases, concern for the quality of the service delivered (the care given to clients) becomes elevated considerably, because of worry that the for-profit sector may emphasize costs rather than service quality.

## Examples

Examples of governments exiting from service without retaining some major participation, such as a major regulatory responsibility or contracting, are rare except for hospitals. There are many examples, however, in the human services, such as in day care or homes for the aged, where state or local governments have opted not to deliver the service but to purchase it when needed. And there is a very extensive private, nonprofit sector, such as charitable agencies, that already provides help to citizens.

**For-Profit Examples.** An unusual example of giving up a service to the for-profit private sector comes from France, where city building inspections, other than for fire safety, have been delegated to private industry. In the French Civil Code, builders are liable for damages for ten years on a structure and two years on secondary components, and, thus, builders take out insurance. French insurance companies in turn hire building inspectors to determine if insured buildings are sound. The French government depends on the economic incentives of the insurance industry to maintain safety.[7]

Public hospitals have been sold or leased to private for-profit firms on a number of occasions. The Hospital Corporation of America (HCA) owns or leases more than twenty-five hospitals previously owned or controlled by municipalities.[8] In Fort Pierce, Florida, HCA used its own capital to rebuild after a local referendum failed. The city subsequently contracted with HCA for services. Property taxes are paid on the hospital. Other private firms also own various hospitals. Prince George's County, Maryland, recently proposed to lease two hospitals and an ambulatory care facility to a private firm. The government would receive funds from the purchase of operating assets, annual rent, property tax payments, and a share of profits in excess of the corporation's usual annual profit margin. This agreement would have required the continuation of community services and indigent care at present levels. The county would review rates. The firm had agreed to employ all employees of the county's hospital system and provide comparable or better fringe benefits to the employees as well as to give them credit for prior years of service.[9] The County Council rejected the plan after considerable objections were raised by segments of the public, especially over possible reduction in care for the poor and elderly.

Probably the major problem in privatizing public hospitals is the problem of caring for indigents. As the principal source of medical care to the indigent, county hospitals provide both ambulatory and inpatient care for people whether or not they have any source of payment for their care. County hospitals take all comers, and these hospitals are a resource for treating indigent patients when private hospitals and doctors fail to provide adequate care or require prior assurance of the ability to pay.[10] Public hospitals therefore are often left with mainly uninsured, low-revenue-producing patients.

Between 1966 and 1977, California reduced the number of its county hospitals from sixty-four to fifty-one by closure, sale, lease, or transfer. Since 1977, additional counties have closed their hospitals and two of these counties (Santa Barbara and Tulare) are paying for care of their indigent patients in private hospitals or in the public hospitals of neighboring counties.[11]

In the United States as a whole in 1971, approximately 12.4 percent of the 4,800 community hospitals were for-profit, with 30.6 percent being public, and the remaining 57 percent private non-profit.[12]

One author in discussing hospital costs has stated:

> Arguments that the private sector can do the job better and cheaper often win instant agreement without any requirement for substantiating the claim. As far as health care is concerned, there is little evidence to support that position. A study of California's Medi-Cal costs found county hospitals to be about 5 percent less expensive than the average California hospital, and when differences between hospitals were adjusted for the case mix of their patients' diagnoses, county hospitals were about 8 percent below average. The ready acceptance of arguments in favor of private efficiency and frugality in the absence of solid supporting evidence illustrates the ideological nature of the debate.[13]

Erie County, New York, in the midst of a budget crisis, attempted to negotiate the sale of its public hospital to private owners, but public opposition and a hospital workers strike stymied the plan. Opposition was based on the fear that adequate services to indigents would not be provided in the private facility and by workers' apprehension that their salary level would be reopened for negotiation.[14]

The city of Detroit transferred the Detroit General Hospital to a private hospital consortium in 1980. There was considerable negotiation on the terms of the transfer. The consortium accepted the current salary levels of transferred employees but won the right to renegotiate fringe benefits. Within six months after the transfer, the number of licensed beds was reduced by 45 percent and the number of hospital employees reduced by 15 percent. Part of the reduction seemed to reflect reduced service provision, but most represented closer attention to operating costs. The consortium agreed to maintain a full service, acute-care medical center only after the state agreed to reimburse the hospital for the costs of indigent patients not covered by federal Medicaid.[15]

**Nonprofit Examples.** In human services areas a frequently cited example of a nonprofit facility is the House of Umoja in Philadelphia, which since 1972 has acted as an extended family for youth and a place for mediating differences among warring youth gangs. It reports success in reducing gang violence, from 35 deaths in 1974 to one in 1977. The agency also provides escort programs for the elderly and assistance in installing locks for elderly and female-headed households. Both programs are aimed at reducing crime and improving prospects for economic development.[16] Similar examples are Jeff-Vander-Lou, Inc. in St. Louis, a neighborhood group that has constructed more than 732 units of housing, facilities for the elderly, and day care centers, and has developed manufacturing service programs that employ hundreds of neighborhood people; and Homes for Black Children in Detroit, which reports having placed more children in permanent homes than all of Detroit's thirteen public and private agencies combined.[17]

A third example is the Cenikor Foundation, Inc., a nonprofit agency established in 1968 in Denver (with branches in Fort Worth and Houston) that provides drug, alcohol, and criminal rehabilitation. Approximately 70 percent of the clients are referred from the core system of social service agencies; the remaining 30 percent arrive as walk-ins. Program graduates often become staff; 40 percent of the agency's funding consists of contributions from foundations and corporations, with 60 percent coming from revenues of Cenikor's own businesses. The agency receives no federal or state funding. Its residents are employed in its own service stations, snow removal service, residential landscaping, and other endeavors. It reports that 70 percent of persons who have been in its three-year program have not returned to the penal system.[18]

These three examples are groups that have formed independently of government rather than being directly encouraged by them. They have not arisen in situations where the government actually withdrew from the service. The question here, however, is whether local government can encourage such activity and how (without undue interference or regulations).

A potential option for a local government is to give up operation of recreational and cultural facilities such as museums and zoos, though in some cases, as in Oakland, the purpose is primarily to alleviate cash flow problems. The Oakland facility is being sold to a private group with a lease-back arrangement so that the city still operates the facility.

The city of Buffalo in 1976 transferred its zoo to the Buffalo Zoological Society, a private, nonprofit organization, though it is responsible for a portion of the zoo's operating deficit.[19] Many jurisdictions in New Jersey, Ohio, and other states have sold their sewer and water systems and electrical utilities to private companies or to new independent authorities.

Finally, a classic example of a potential government exit is all-volunteer fire departments. But this author knows of no cases where any city of any size has switched from public fire protection to all-volunteer departments. Most volunteer departments are in locations where fire protection started as a volunteer program, and these are usually in rural jurisdictions.

## Evaluation

**Cost of Government Service.** To the extent that the government can withdraw from an activity, government costs can decline substantially. Administrative costs could occur to the extent that special close-out costs are involved, as when government employees have to be laid off. The motivation for the governments to transfer a government facility to a private organization is generally to reduce expenditures. Most of the transfers identified as examples were in services that were not self-financing but required, when operated by the government, significant general revenues by the local government. Transfer of the function would give immediate relief to the government's general budget. In some cases, the local government first attempted to transfer the service responsibility to a higher level of government. Only when this effort failed did the local government consider transfer or sale to the private sector.[20]

**Cost to Citizens.** These arrangements can reduce the cost to citizens, both through reduced taxes and through use of lesser paid personnel, and in the case of nonprofit agencies, volunteers. This approach may not increase competition, however, at least not in those cases where the government gives up a facility such as a hospital or zoo. Especially if the agency is a for-profit firm, the real possibility exists that in the long run the organization will increase client fees over what they would have been if the government had continued to operate the facility. In a number of the transfers described earlier, the private owner raised charges for the services provided by the facility. This may, however, not be because of more costly operations or the desire to increase profits but may represent an attempt to recoup the amount by which the government had previously subsidized the hospital care rates.

As discussed under "Franchises," substantial evidence indicates that giving up solid waste collection is likely to make the service more expensive. Studies of private collection versus contracting out by the government versus use of government employees have found that purely private collection is the most expensive. Both the Savas and the Kemper and Quigley studies found that the price of private collection "is significantly greater," with Kemper and Quigley estimating the price of private collection to be 25 percent–36 percent higher than the cost of municipal service. They conclude with the recommendation that cities should provide the service themselves but should contract to private firms under competitive bidding. Savas suggests that the reasons for the higher costs of private firms are that these firms incur higher billing costs, experience more bad debts, and incur inefficient service routes.[21] And as noted earlier, one study of Medi-Cal in California found that county hospitals were about 8 percent less costly than the average California hospital. These findings are far from conclusive, but they do provide a warning about overexpectations that privatization will lead to substantially lowered costs to clients.

Client groups, particularly low-income groups, probably can fare better under government ownership to the extent that the government subsidizes those costs and would not do so to the same extent in a transfer.

**Choices Available to Clients.** The amount of choice will vary. If a private firm reduces the accessibility of the facility (such as hospitals) to certain clients (such as low-income clients), choice is reduced. If, however, private firms attempt to broaden the appeal of the service, more choices would develop.

**Quality/Effectiveness of Service.** There are many claims on both sides but little empirical evidence. Where a profit-making firm takes over responsibility for activities, there is likely to be more emphasis on profit-making than on service quality, and, potentially, quality could diminish. It would be highly instructive to look at the numerous examples of private hospital takeovers, to examine the effects on fees and service quality for government versus nonprofit private versus private for-profit operations.

Nonprofit private human service agencies claim that substantial gains in effectiveness have been achieved. The claims seldom appear to have been examined objectively and systematically by an independent agency. However, it seems likely that the service providers will be more personally caring, even if not as well trained professionally. Per dollar, it seems likely that service quality can increase. More of a problem, however, is whether a sufficient number of these agencies exist to handle the load often faced by urban area government human service agencies. Are there enough capable, caring individuals who are willing to work at low wages or put in time as volunteer workers? This is a major unknown.

**Distributional Effects.** In arrangements involving for-profit firms, it is possible, if not likely, that rates will increase to reflect the extra cost-consciousness of the firm. The evidence cited earlier suggests that this does occur. Increased rates will work particularly to the disadvantage of low-income persons unless some form of subsidy is used. If a government gives up a service, leaving it to community groups or private firms, the effects depend partly on the ability of households or associations to provide that service themselves.

For hospitals, it is not clear that governments between counties and private organizations taking over hospitals can guarantee that indigent persons will be served and not discouraged from seeking care. Empirical research in communities affected by public hospital closures could help answer this question.

**Staying Power and Potential for Service Disruption.** The switch to fully private sector delivery introduces more uncertainty than delivery by government. Private for-profit firms can go out of business and probably face a larger potential for strikes and financial problems. Private nonprofit agencies depend on the inspiration of their top leadership for prolonged continuity. Nevertheless, many private agencies, and of course, many business firms stay in business for many years.

**Feasibility.** Government withdrawal from a service presents major feasibility questions. This approach is probably the most radical of all the approaches. Most proposals will encounter substantial opposition from interest groups, including government employees and their associations and client groups, such as disadvantaged groups, that fear the arrangement will hurt them. Seldom will such proposals satisfy all interested parties.

Certain forms of this approach will be considerably more feasible than others, particularly those that build on existing private agencies and do not involve a complete withdrawal of the government from a service. This approach is most feasible when pursued in the context of avoiding an expansion in government services rather than a complete exit of government from an existing service. Finally, there is the problem of finding a private organization that is willing to take over the government service. Often in the past, in situations involving the nonprofit private sector, the private parties themselves have created the private agency. If governments begin explicitly to search for existing agencies to encourage them to take over responsibility, the search is likely to take a considerable amount of time and effort.

**Overall Impact.** This approach is likely to achieve the largest government cost savings when it can be done. Nevertheless, there is likely to be considerable opposition, depending on how substantial the proposal is. A government that is voluntarily giving up a service will likely attempt to retain some form of control, even if only to assure interest groups that certain minimum types and levels of service will be provided.

Debates over the proper role of government and over its efficiency and effectiveness compared to the private sector will certainly arise over proposals for this approach. Empirical evidence that could enlighten the debate is quite limited; the evidence available to date gives mixed findings.

# CHAPTER 10

# DEMARKETING/REDUCING THE DEMAND FOR SERVICE

## Definition and Rationale

In this approach, a government attempts to reduce demand or the need for services, through a variety of marketing techniques. The government undertakes to encourage potential clients of services to alter their behavior in a constructive way so as to lessen the need for future services.

The rationale here is that in some situations the amount of government service needed can be reduced by private actions, with the results of reducing government costs and, in some cases, improving the well-being of the citizens.

Demand reduction can also be attempted more directly by using some of the other approaches, such as the use of fees and charges and regulation.

## Examples

Some examples are as follows:

- Prince George's County, Maryland, has a public education campaign to explain to county residents the purpose and proper use of the county's ambulance system. Since the public education campaign was instituted, the number of unnecessary ambulance responses was reduced from more than 50 percent of the total to 22 percent of the total.[1]

- The city of Tucson has had public campaigns to reduce the use of water. The Washington [D.C.] Suburban Sanitary Commission has had a similar campaign to conserve water.

- There have been widespread efforts to encourage the public to carpool to avoid a variety of direct and indirect public transportation costs.

- Governments have used programs to reduce smoking in bed and to encourage households and businesses to install smoke detectors, fire alarms, and/or sprinkler systems to reduce future fire protection costs. Local governments may also require such actions by use of their regulatory authority.

- Campaigns can be undertaken regularly to encourage personal well-being and health care, such as encouraging exercise programs that are likely to reduce future physical and mental health care needs.

- Local governments could encourage networks of people to help each other in their community—perhaps through neighborhood associations, churches, schools, social and fraternal organizations, labor unions, and service clubs to reduce the future amount of public assistance needed.

- Governments can undertake publicity programs to educate the public in the use of the 911 emergency number. For New York City, an estimate was made that 700 patrol car dispatches per day are for unnecessary 911 calls.[2]

- There have been campaigns to encourage citizens to reduce litter, separate their solid waste, and deliver certain types of waste to recycling centers—both to reduce trash collection costs and to obtain recyclable products.

- The virtures of off-peak travel can be publicized (particularly if the government also has off-peak rate differentials), reducing government congestion-handling costs. Similarly, a better job of reporting public transit (bus) schedules and locations could be undertaken to achieve lower per-capita cost and increased revenue.

# Evaluation

**Cost of Government Service.** The explicit intent of these de-mand-reducing approaches is to reduce the cost of services. For the most part these efforts tend to be relatively small-scale and probably will yield only small cost reductions. But each small cost savings helps. Perhaps with some ingenuity, substantial demand-reducing ideas can be generated.

Costs are associated with undertaking whatever marketing and publicity effort is required. In general these costs should be small. Public service announcements can be made inexpensively through public service presentations (e.g., on television), though more elab-orate presentations, such as those related to transit systems, can involve substantial costs.

**Cost to Citizens.** Sometimes these demand-reducing options require citizens to make purchases they might not otherwise make, such as smoke detectors or running shoes. The nature of these op-tions, however, is that they are voluntary and are likely to be low cost. In many cases, the result will be worth the cost to the citizens.

**Choices Available to Clients.** This approach does not aim at increasing choice. Rather, it encourages citizens to make certain choices that it is hoped will advance their own personal welfare as well as reduce the cost of government.

**Quality/Effectiveness of Service.** There should be no adverse effects from the client's viewpoint in the quality of service required. In a sense, this approach often is a way to improve service effec-tiveness by increasing citizens' well-being and permitting govern-ments to focus on less avoidable problems.

**Distributional Effects.** Those demarketing efforts aimed at helping citizens (e.g., preventing problems for the citizen) will be of most help to people who have ready access to the publicity media used by the government. Thus, the approach would have less effect on low-income, disadvantaged groups. However, a well-developed program could be tailored to meet the needs of such groups.

**Staying Power and Potential for Service Disruption.** Such campaigns are more likely to be ad hoc than continuous, though there is no inherent reason for this. No undesirable service disrup-tion should occur from this option.

**Feasibility.** The main problems are in developing appropriate demand-reducing efforts. Some marketing publicity could be controversial if not done carefully. Properly done, however, such efforts are likely to be feasible without raising much opposition, and they should be possible at low cost.

**Overall Impact.** These demand-reducing techniques provide an opportunity for governments to be innovative and use business-type marketing and publicity skills not often employed by government agencies. They are not likely, in most cases, to yield substantial cost savings to the government, although on occasion this could occur.

# CHAPTER 11

# OBTAINING TEMPORARY HELP FROM PRIVATE FIRMS

## Definition and Rationale

In this approach, private firms loan personnel, facilities, or equipment, or even provide funds to the local government.

The rationale for loaned-executive programs (or loans of other personnel) is clear. Business executives have knowledge and experience that local managers may lack, or at least the former have a fresh perspective and their experiences are transferable to the problems of government. The rationale for gifts of facilities, equipment, or funds is that the government has been unable to raise sufficient funds for items or activities that the givers believe would be helpful and do not represent a conflict of interest (with possible subsequent legal problems) for the givers. The firm considers the help to be in the community's interest, and it improves the public image of the firm.

## Examples

A relatively common example is the use of loaned executives in a number of local (and state) governments. With loaned-executive programs, business firms loan staff for limited periods of time, such as three to six months, to review local or state government operations and suggest improvements.

A number of cities have recently attempted to obtain resources from the private sector for their recreation programs. In 1980, the city of Detroit issued a "Detroit Recreation Gifts Catalog" as part of its "Recreation Department Partners Programs." Individuals, community groups, businesses, and foundations were invited by the department and the Detroit Chamber of Commerce to purchase tax-deductible items for the city, items that the city could not afford to purchase. The brochure listed such items as equipment (swings, slides, facilities, benches, and bike racks), donations to sponsor city events (senior citizen arts and crafts show, adoption of a sports team, and purchase of trees and shrubs). In 1980, New York City officials in the park department persuaded four corporations located near Madison Square Park to contribute a total of $32,500 toward the park's maintenance. The city used the money to hire a private con-tractor to supplement the bare-bones housekeeping already provided by park agency staff. In 1979, the California East Bay Regional Park District received help from one corporation to "adopt" an 88-acre recreation area. The corporation provided $15,000 in seed money and made a commitment to provide an additional $100,000 over the next three years.[1]

A variation of this option is to establish an agency to act as a clearinghouse for donations of funds, labor, and materials that go to the government. Tulsa, Oklahoma, and San Francisco, California, have done this for park and recreation programs.[2] Dallas firms con-tributed $8 million toward construction of a major $40 million cen-tral research library, long delayed for lack of public funds. An ad hoc friends of Dallas Public Library Committee handled the dona-tions.[3] Another recent example is Baltimore's Blue Chip-In effort to find private financing for, and participation in, a number of city projects previously funded by the federal government. The city hopes to raise $500,000 in the first year for a jobs program. A private, nonprofit foundation was established to give participating busi-nesses a tax write-off. The Mayor's Office of Manpower Resources handles all hiring and monitors each project (such as landscaping, meals for the elderly, recreation programs, public housing, and weatherization for the city's needy families). Firms may also provide some of their own resources—for example, training former CETA workers to provide free, home energy-audit help.[4] Prince George's County, Maryland, is working to establish a private nonprofit arts council to receive tax-exempt contributions from business and in-dividuals. The council would help cultural organizations improve the quality of their events and assist them with financial management and fund raising.[5]

Another fairly common arrangement is for large developers to underwrite major improvements, which, though not required by the local government, would improve access to their facilities. Dallas and Orange County, California, have followed this approach.[6]

## Evaluation

**Cost of Government Service.** Donations will help keep government costs down. Administration costs are generally small, but if the city has to undertake considerable effort to receive funds, such as establishing a nonprofit foundation, this could add administrative costs (though the private sector itself might take on the burden of establishing these nonprofit agencies). Establishing new nonprofit agencies to raise contributions seems to be a common practice; their major purpose is to assure that such contributions are tax exempt. Savings to the public are offset somewhat when donations are used as offsets to local taxes and thereby reduce government revenues.

Although many loaned-executive programs (including those for state governments) have been used, outside evaluations of their success in actually producing savings are lacking. Final reports from these programs typically identify dozens, if not hundreds, of suggested improvements and make estimates of potential savings for each. Implementation of suggestions, however, usually is difficult and probably would take much more time and cost than recognized when the estimates of potential savings are made. Although these programs likely produce net savings to the government, the savings probably are much less than those projected in the final reports.

**Cost to Citizens.** These programs can be expected to reduce costs by helping government keep costs down. Their overall effect, however, is likely to be minor.

**Choices Available to Clients.** This approach does not inherently alter client choice, other than by permitting activities that otherwise would not be available without the contributions.

**Quality/Effectiveness of Service.** Again there is no inherent effect, other than whatever improvements in service quality are generated by the donations.

**Distributional Effects.** This is not likely to be an important concern with this approach. However, to the extent that the help from the private sector is directed at helping low-income families (such as the Baltimore effort), or some other group, it will be more helpful to that group. Loaned-executive programs probably affect citizens generally, rather than affecting any one particular client group.

**Staying Power and Potential for Service Disruption.** These types of donations are essentially ad hoc and temporary. Governments cannot depend upon them for prolonged periods of time. Annual programs of donations will likely be subject to interruption unless considerable effort is undertaken to sustain the program. In any case, firms will typically prefer to make contributions to nongovernmental agencies, since governments have their own revenue-raising authority.

**Feasibility.** Though small-scale contributions can usually be obtained, at least at times when the local government clearly has scarce resources, it is likely to be difficult to sustain major continuing contributions. The level and number of contributions will depend on the financial condition of private businesses and certainly will be reduced in recessionary and difficult times. The contributions will also depend on the particular interest and leadership in those companies.

Legal problems exist in establishing a mechanism for providing such contributions on a tax-deductible basis, resulting in potentially complicated arrangements, such as the establishment of a special tax-exempt foundation to receive the funds.

**Overall Impact.** This approach is not likely to provide a major continuing source of resources for service delivery, because the approach is too dependent upon the voluntary generosity and ability of private firms to make donations. The incentives are altruism, tax deductibility, and the desire to maintain an attractive community image, but it is not generally the business of private firms to make contributions to governments.

# CHAPTER 12

# USING FEES AND CHARGES TO ADJUST DEMAND

## Definition and Rationale

Here, users of a service are charged a fee based on the amount of their use of the government-supplied activity, thus putting the financial burden on users of the activity.[1] This report is not concerned with the use of fees and charges for the sake of raising revenues but rather with their use for adjusting the amount of service demanded by individual citizens or private organizations and, thus, affecting the cost of services. The use of fees and charges has been increasing in recent years, especially in areas affected by state fiscal containment efforts.[2] The major purpose of those fees, however, has been to raise revenues.

The rationale of this approach is that the persons who use a particular service should pay for it, in accordance with their amount of use. This should cause people to consider the service's cost to them and to adjust their demand for the service in proportion to the value they set on that service. This, then, more closely approximates the business principle of being able to sell to citizens only those services that citizens want. When fees are charged, many citizens can be expected to reduce their use of the service from the level of use when the service represented no added cost to them (which occurs if an activity is funded out of general revenues). The use of general revenues, such as the property tax, drives up the demand for, and consumption of, services since there is no added cost to the consumer and thus no incentive to conserve.

An additional advantage of fees and charges is that they give better signals to government managers about the needed size of public facilities. For example, if large numbers of citizens are using a service when the charge for the service is close to the cost of producing it, then it is more likely to be appropriate to add additional facilities.

Fees and charges are applicable to a specific service to the extent that usage by individual customers can be distinguished and charges can be related to individual uses.

The key to the ability to use fees and charges is that specific beneficiaries receive the service, and the service can be divided among them without a substantial number of free riders who escape the charges but nevertheless receive benefits. Another way of expressing this is that the service should be private rather than collective, that is, there are specific identifiable users, and those not paying for the time can be excluded from the benefits. Fees and charges are, thus, potentially applicable to services provided to individuals, as listed in exhibit 4.

Charges can be used to ration demand only if the client controls the demand. Charges such as monthly garbage collection charges and assessments per front foot for street sweeping, cleaning, and street repairs are not demand-affecting charges. These are primarily revenue-raising devices. Once someone moves into a house, the charge for that lot no longer rations demand; subsequently, the cost to the household does not vary, regardless of how much waste or water is generated by the household. The front lot charge can, however, conceivably affect house-purchase decisions.

Governments can develop fees and charges based not only on quantity of use but also on the timing of that use (to encourage off-peak usage and thus reduce expensive capacity requirements, as with transportation and water). Fees and charges can conceptually take into account other cost-generating characteristics of the services, such as location; for example, larger fees can be charged for water and sewer connections located in sparsely settled parts of the community where the costs of capital facilities and maintenance are expected to be higher. Such charging arrangements would tend to encourage the private sector to request services in less costly areas of the community (and at least costly times of the day). Another example used in some cities, such as Fort Worth, Texas, is to give citizens a choice between levels of service, for example, different fees for different levels of garbage collection: backdoor or curbside.

Finally, a drawback to switching from taxes and fees and charges is that the latter are not deductible for residents who itemize their deductions for federal income tax purposes.

## Examples

Classic examples of fees and charges occur for special recreational activities (such as golf courses, tennis courts, and swimming pools) and for water use. In the latter case, the charge depends on metering the use of the water supply by individual customers. For recreational activities involving open parks, entrance fees have seldom (if ever) been charged at the local level, and libraries have not charged entrance fees. Services of police and fire departments tend to be collective, though in recent years proposals for fees and charges for some activities have been proposed, such as charging for calls made or charging for false alarms (fire or police).

Local governments have increasingly charged developers for the costs of new infrastructure generated by their projects. For example, in Corvallis, Oregon, housing developers now must meet much of the cost of extending the city's water system before they build.[3] To the extent that such charges ration demand, they are relevant to the discussion here. For example, Snohomish County, Washington (population 337,000) has different developer road charges, depending on the expected congestion level and expected road costs. This approach can encourage developers to build in less costly areas.[4]

Exhibit 5 lists recent applications of fees and charges. This list does not cover all activities for which fees and charges have been proposed or used.

## Evaluation

**Cost of Government Service.** The purpose of the fees and charges discussed here is to reduce service cost by reducing the amount of demand and consumption that would occur without added costs to citizens for using the service. Thus far, however, the author has not found specific studies that provide empirical evidence for the extent to which, after the introduction of fees and charges, service costs have actually declined. Many examples should exist, particularly for recent years, from which useful evidence could be obtained.

Exhibit 5. TYPES OF FEES, CHARGES, AND LICENSES

**Police protection**
special patrol service fees
parking fees and charges
fees for fingerprints, copies
payments for extra police service
  at stadiums, theaters, circuses

**Transportation**
subway and bus fares
bridge tolls
landing and departure fees
hangar rentals
concession rentals
parking meter receipts

**Health and hospitals**
inoculation charges
X-ray charges
hospital charges, including per diem
  rates and service charges
ambulance charges
concession rentals

**Education**
charges for books
charges for gymnasium uniforms
  or special equipment
concession rentals

**Recreation**
greens fees
parking charges
concession rentals
admission fees or charges
permit charges for tennis
  courts, etc.
charges for specific
  recreation services
picnic stove fees
stadium gate tickets
stadium club fees
park development charges

**Sanitation**
domestic and commercial trash
  collection fees
industrial waste charges

**Sewerage**
sewerage system fees

**Other public
utility operations**
water meter permits
water service charges
electricity rates
telephone booth rentals

## Housing, neighborhood and commercial development

street tree fees
tract map filing fees
street-lighting installations
convention center revenues—
  event charges
  scoreboard fees
  hall and meeting room leases
  concessions

## Commodity sales

salvage materials
sales of maps
sales of codes

## Licenses and fees

advertising vehicle
amusements (ferris wheels, etc.)
billiard and pool
bowling alley
circus and carnival
coal dealers
commercial combustion
dances
dog tags
duplicate dog tags
electrician—first class
electrician—second class
film storage
foot peddler
hucksters and itinerant peddlers
heating equipment contractors
junk dealer
loading zone permit
lumber dealer
pawnbrokers
plumbers—first class
plumbers—second class

pest eradicator
poultry dealer
produce dealer—itinerant
pushcart
rooming house and hotel
secondhand dealer
secondhand auto dealer
sign inspection
solicitation
shooting gallery
taxi
taxi transfer license
taxi driver
theaters
trees—Christmas
vending—coin
vault cleaners
sound truck
refuse hauler
land fill
sightseeing bus
wrecking license

SOURCE: Selma J. Mushkin and Charles L. Vehorn, "User Fees and Charges," *Governmental Finance* (November 1977), p. 48.

Administrative billing and collection costs for fees and charges can be considerable. For example, for charges based on the amount of water used, the agency must purchase, install, and maintain meters at each customer's location, as well as provide for reading the meters, billing, and collection. In some cases, however, these administrative costs may be relatively small, as in water supply. Little documented information on the administrative cost of switching to fees and charges exists.

**Cost to Citizens.** Theoretically, reduced use of a service should lead to lower tax bills. Consumers' actual cost for the service then depends on the amount they use (and are charged for). In actual practice, since fees and charges are most often used as a revenue-raising device, citizens could actually end up paying more (both the old tax and added charges).

A major concern with fees and charges is that they are not deductible for federal income tax purposes, as are property and sales tax. Thus, for those households that itemize their deductions, the switch to fees and charges is likely to mean increased taxes. The result would be increased net cost to those households unless cost savings because of lower use of the service were enough to offset this federal tax increase.

**Choices Available to Clients.** With fees and charges, the individual potential customer is faced with more choices, now that the customer has to pay for usage. The customer now has the opportunity to make less use of a service rather than paying a bill whose size is independent of the amount of use.

**Quality/Effectiveness of the Service.** Though fees and charges do not directly affect service quality, the customer has the opportunity to express concern over quality through nonuse. If an agency finds revenues dropping, it has the opportunity to find out why and to determine whether customers are reducing use because of poor quality or for some other reasons.

**Distributional Effects.** This is probably the central concern for communities considering fees and charges. At first glance, it would appear that fees and charges generally would adversely affect low-income families. For example, the fees and charges for use of drinking water would likely absorb a higher proportion of those families' income than would be the case for middle- and upper-income families. But, as noted, higher-income families that itemize deductions may also resist fees and charges because of the federal tax implications. A few studies have been done on the distributional effects of various user charges.[5] Fixed-rate charges (e.g., a fixed sum per month) are likely to be regressive, whereas charges based on amount of use or the timing and locational characteristics of use may not be regressive, or at least may be less regressive. The argument is that high-income people tend to live in larger homes, at lower density, and at more distant locations and so have higher costs of services; if the charges are constructed properly, they will have higher user charges. With fixed-rate user charges that are primarily for revenue-raising purposes and not really part of privatization proposals, low-income people could, however, end up paying more than the cost of serving them, since their use may be less frequent and less costly.[6]

**Staying Power and Potential for Service Disruption.** Fees and charges are not likely to cause service disruption since the delivery is still being undertaken by the governmental agency. Once fees and charges have been introduced, they are likely to remain in effect for at least a number of years. If the charges are readily relatable to the amount of use and are easily understood by the public, they will probably continue in effect.

**Feasibility.** Fees and charges to affect demand are not feasible for collective services. For other services, legal issues may require review of each individual case. Fees from developers to cover costs of related new infrastructure have raised legal problems. If a local government can show a reasonable relationship between the cost of the service and the charge, these charges probably will pass the legal test.[7]

A recent Advisory Commission on Intergovernmental Relations (*ACIR*) survey provides evidence of the current salability of fees and charges. A nationwide survey found 55 percent of the respondents felt that "charges for specific services" was the best way for local governments to raise needed additional revenues.[8] And in a December 1981 survey, 45 percent of responding local governments reported no opposition to increases in fees and charges.[9]

**Overall Impact.** Not enough empirical evidence exists to determine whether the introduction of fees and charges would lead to significantly reduced costs to the government and customers. Governments can probably increase fees and charges more readily than general taxes. Since such fees and charges are presumably based on actual costs, increases should be easier to justify to the public.

The overall advantage to the government may not be reductions in actual local expenditures but rather the degree to which expenditures can be directly related to revenues and the ability to be more sensitive to demand. However, without well-constructed fees and charges (related to important cost-affecting variables), charges can easily become regressive.

# CHAPTER 13

# CONCLUSIONS AND RECOMMENDATIONS

In these times of shifting priorities and highly restricted government revenues, it seems imperative that communities consider options to reduce government expenditures but without being detrimental to the community.

The options addressed in this report are important ones for governments to consider. They each come in many variations and applications. They can be used in various combinations. Some are likely to have only small impacts, but all should be considered by local governments; even minor cost reductions are helpful.

Exhibit 6 summarizes the author's judgment of each approach's impact ("on the average"), based on the highly limited evidence.[1] Probably the options that can have major impacts on government costs are use of franchises, encouragement of private agencies to take over an activity or service, and use of regulatory and tax authority. But these are major actions requiring major effort to implement. And these will not necessarily reduce significantly the costs of services to clients. Contracting and self-help also can be quite attractive as cost-reduction opportunities. Following are ten recommendations for communities.

**1. Encourage Officials to Take on a More Entrepreneurial Role.** Officials, both elected and appointed, and service managers

Exhibit 6. EVALUATION OF IMPACTS

| Approach | Reduce Cost of Government | Reduce Cost to Clients | Increase Client Choice | Improve or Maintain Service Quality | Likelihood of Major Distributional Effects | Added Likelihood of Disruption of Service | Difficulty in Implementation | Overall Impact |
|---|---|---|---|---|---|---|---|---|
| *Government agencies retain the primary responsibility* | | | | | | | | |
| Contracting[a] | 2[b] | 2 | 0 | ? | N[e] | Y | Some | 2 |
| Volunteers | 1[b] | 1 | 0 | ? | N | N | Little | 1 |
| Demarketing | 1 | 0[c] | 0 | 2 | N | N | Little | 1 |
| Temporary help | 1 | 1 | 0 | 1 | N | N | Little | 1 |
| Fees and charges to adjust demand | 1 | ?[d] | 2 | 1 | Y[e] | N | Some | 1 |
| *Private units take primary responsibility* | | | | | | | | |
| Franchise[a] | 3[b] | ? | 2 | ? | Y | Y | Considerable | ? |
| Grants/subsidies | 1 | ? | ? | ? | ? | Y | Some | ? |
| Vouchers | ? | ? | 3 | 1 | Y | Y | Great | ? |
| Self-help | 2 | 1 | 2 | 2 | ? | Y | ? | 1 |
| Regulation (deregulation)/taxing | 1 | 2 | 1 | 2 | ? | N | Considerable | 2 |
| Encouraging private takeover | 3 | 1 | ? | 2 | N | ? | Some | 2 |
| Nonprofit | 3 | ? | ? | ? | Y | Y | Considerable | ? |
| Profit organizations[a] | | | | | | | | |

a. For these approaches, the extent of cost savings to the government and/or citizens will depend considerably on whether there are multiple suppliers. If there are multiple suppliers, cost savings are more likely to develop.

b. 1,2,3 = the effort is likely, on the average, to have a small (1), medium (2), large (3) impact.

c. 0 = the approach is, in general, likely to have a neutral impact.

d. ? = impact not at all clear; largely depends on the specific application.

e. Y/N = yes/no.

should take on a new, broader role. They should be encouraged to think and act as community service providers and overseers, and not solely as service deliverers. They should consider a wide spectrum of alternatives to public service delivery. This does not mean that public officials will become agents to break up local government but rather that opportunities involving substantial departures from normal service delivery practices should be fully explored. This also means that government managers need to increase their policy formulation, negotiation, and monitoring skills.

**2. Alter Incentives for Managers.** This new role requires that governments alter incentives for managers. Rewards should be available to managers that identify cost-effective alternatives even though those alternatives reduce the manager's number of employees and budget. At the same time, governments should not neglect opportunities for internal improvements such as those listed below the double line in exhibit 1. The incentive issue has already arisen in jurisdictions attempting to encourage managers to improve internal productivity. A number of local governments have attempted to relate management compensation to performance. Governments need to reward managers for reducing government expenditures, whether the reductions are accomplished internally or by privatization. Performance, however, should also be assessed as to its impact on the community's citizens. Merely recommending shedding of an activity without concern for community welfare is not appropriate.

**3. Establish an Ongoing Service Delivery Review System.** Communities should establish an ongoing review system that periodically, perhaps every three to four years, examines the efficiency and quality of each government activity. Since it will not be feasible to examine each government activity each year, services should probably be examined on a staggered basis. Each activity needs to be examined in detail, using evaluation criteria such as those used in this report. This review effort can itself have a beneficial effect on service delivery. It introduces a form of competition and motivation, especially to the current delivery agent (whether public or private), to provide better quality or less expensive performance.

**4. Focus Reviews on Individual Services.** Such reviews probably should be on a service basis rather than focusing on an approach basis. Each service activity should be the subject of a separate review, with each alternative approach considered for that particular service.

**5. Include Government Managers and Citizen Representatives on Review Teams.** Review teams can include citizen representatives, but government managers should be an integral part of the review teams. The participants may not end up agreeing on the best approach, but their dialogue will be likely to bring out the major arguments and evidence on all sides.

**6. Before Switching, Give the Current Delivery Mechanism an Opportunity to Improve.** If the service component appears inefficient or ineffective, the agency should consider other forms of service delivery. But it should first give the current delivery organization the opportunity to improve.

**7. Introduce Competitive Elements.** More competition should be introduced wherever practical to motivate service delivery organizations to provide less expensive or more effective services. Competitive-type contracts or private versus public competition could be used to accomplish that end.

**8. Increase Amount and Dissemination of Evaluative Information.** Considerable need exists for more evaluative information and more information sharing on current applications of these approaches. There are numerous "natural experiments" going on throughout the country. Other communities could benefit from knowing about them. The information provided should include details of the way an approach was implemented, its scope, problems that occurred and how they were worked out (or not worked out), and more substantive information on the actual impacts (cost, quality, and the distribution of effects among the community's client groups). It is highly desirable that information on inputs be obtained for periods beyond the first year after the approach is introduced to identify actual longer-term impacts. Information sharing should not be limited to descriptions, anecdotal information, and projections of future cost savings.

Preferably, local jurisdictions in an area would cooperate in an information-sharing effort through an organization such as the Council of Governments. Each government, and individual agencies within each government, should provide systematic documentation of their experiments, including failures as well as successes. This information should be organized and disseminated by service to provide information to functional managers, such as public works or police managers.

**9. Make A Special Effort to Maintain Morale of Employees.** Government should make special efforts to maintain the morale and productivity of government employees during cutback reviews and actions. Employees should not be made the scapegoat for problems in cost containment that occur because of government rules, regulations, and decisions by the community and elected officials. Officials should keep employees fully informed on possible actions and provide assistance to employees who lose their jobs through a reduction in force.

**10. Evaluate Actions and Correct Problems.** Finally, within two or three years after introducing a new delivery approach, government managers should evaluate those experiences and take corrective action if those experiences have not met expectations.

Periodic explicit consideration of service delivery options such as those discussed in this report should become a common practice in local (and state) governments. Considering various options will enable governments to use public and private resources for the greatest good of the public.

# NOTES

NOTES TO CHAPTER 1

1. The original version of this report was prepared for the Greater Washington Research Center's "Task Force on Local Government Response to Fiscal Pressure." This report also draws from the author's work for a study undertaken by the International City Management Association for the U.S. Department of Housing and Urban Development on "Alternative Approaches for the Private Delivery of Public Services."

2. For example, a survey of 100 cities in November 1981 by the U.S. Conference of Mayors found that 59 percent stated that they had reduced or would soon have to reduce services. The remainder reported that they had not, but some noted that they had already cut to the bone and could not cut anymore. ("The FY 82 Budget and the Cities: A 100 City Survey," U.S. Conference of Mayors, November 20, 1981, p. 7.)

3. There is considerable variation in the current use of these terms. For this paper, the definitions given in exhibit 2 are intended to limit the meaning of these terms. Often groups using terms such as *voluntarism* and *self-help* will utilize broader definitions.

4. It may very well be that as Mayor George Latimer of St. Paul said in his July 30, 1981, testimony at the U.S. Senate Subcommittee on Intergovernmental Relations Forum on Alternative Service Delivery, that major city revitalization efforts are where new private-public partnership seems to work best. However, these topics are being covered in depth elsewhere in the Task Force's work.

5. For a discussion of this subject, especially from the private, for-profit sector viewpoint, see "Public-Private Partnership: An Opportunity for Urban Communities," Committee for Economic Development, Washington, D.C., February 1982.

6. See, for example, John McKnight, "Professionalized Service and Disabling Help," in *Disabling Professions*, Marion Boyars, Inc., 1978.

7. July 30, 1981, testimony at the U.S. Senate Subcommittee on Intergovernmental Relations Forum on Alternative Service Delivery.

8. John D. Hanrahan, *Government for Sale: Contracting Out the New Patronage*, American Federation of State, County and Municipal Employees, 1977.

NOTES TO CHAPTER 2

1. This type of competition is described in E.S. Savas, "Intra-city Competition Between Public and Private Service Delivery," *Public Administration Review*, January/February 1981.

2. Donald Fisk, Herbert Keisling, and Tom Muller, *Private Provision of Public Services: An Overview*, The Urban Institute, May 1978, pp. 6–9.

3. This becomes especially possible if the government agency routinely contracts out a portion of an activity that agency employees also undertake. The contract prices can be compared to the cost of government service delivery.

4. California Tax Foundation, "Contracting Out Local Government Services in California," May 1981. Responses were received from 92 of 310 cities, counties, and school districts to which questionnaires were sent. Five of the 92 jurisdictions did not contract out (one county, three school districts, and one special district). Most but not all these contracts were with private providers; some were with other goverments or special districts.

5. "Public-Private Partnership: An Opportunity for Urban Communities," Committee for Economic Development, Washington, D.C., February 1982, pp. 67–68.

6. William Shonick and Ruth Roemer, "Private Management of California County Hospitals: Expectations and Performance," School of Public Health, University of California, Los Angeles, February 1982.

7. See Derzon, LeCompte, and Lewin, "Management Contracts Seen as Largely Resolving Needs," *Hospitals*, June 16, 1981.

8. Statement of Louis A. Witzman, President, Rural Metropolitan Fire Department, Inc., to U.S. Senate Subcommittee Intergovernmental Relations Forum on Alternative Service Delivery, July 29, 1981.

9. Roger S. Ahlbrandt, Jr., "Implications of Contracting for a Public Service," *Urban Affairs Quarterly*, March 1974; and "Alternatives to Traditional Public Safety Delivery Systems: Civilians in Public Safety Services," Institute for Local Self Government, September 1977. The latter compared Scottsdale to three other similar cities in Arizona. It found that Scottsdale fire services cost about one-half the cost of services in the other cities.

10. *Fiscal Watchdog*, August 1981, Local Government Center, Santa Barbara, California; and Mark Frazier, "Transatlantic Perspectives," German Marshall Fund, July 1981.

11. *Fiscal Watchdog*, August 1981.

12. *Fiscal Watchdog*, November 1980.

13. "Public-Private Partnership," p. 67.

14. Arnold Gurin and others, "Contracting for Services as a Mechanism for the Delivery of Human Services: A Study of Contracting Practices in Three Human Services Agencies in Massachusetts," Brandeis Univesity, Graduate School for Advanced Studies and Social Welfare, June 1980.

15. Keon S. Chi, "Innovations: Private Contractor Work Release Centers: The Illinois Experience," The Council of State Governments, Lexington, Kentucky, July 1982.

16. *Fiscal Watchdog*, September 1981.

17. Various materials provided by the city of Poughkeepsie, N.Y. See also Daniel B. Breuer and Daniel W. Fitzpatrick, "An Experience in Contracting Out for Services," *Governmental Finance*, March 1980. However, there was a major struggle between the employee association and the city, and recently New York State's Public

Employment Relations Board ordered city officials to offer jobs and back pay to city workers who had lost their jobs.

18. Various materials provided by the city of Phoenix. See also, Mark Hughes, "Contracting Services in Phoenix," *Public Management*, October 1982.

19. Savas, "Intra-city Competition Between Public and Private Service Delivery."

20. Elisha C. Freedman, "A Poor Man's Guide to Restricting Local Government Taxes," in *Proposition 13 and its Consequences for Public Management*, edited by Selma J. Mushkin, Abt Books, 1980, p. 91.

21. "Public-Private Partnership," p. 77.

22. October 26, 1979, Contract for Collection of Residential Refuse Between the Tulsa Energy Resource Recovery Authority [created by the city of Tulsa] and Tulsa Refuse, Inc.

23. "Case Studies in Educational Performance Contracting," 6 vols., R-900, The Rand Corporation, December 1971.

24. "Cost-Cutting Strategies for Park and Recreation Agency," U.S. Department of Interior, Park and Recreation Technical Services, 1981, p. 12.

25. "Cost-Cutting Strategies for Park and Recreation Agency," p. 16.

26. E.S. Savas, "Public vs. Private Refuse Collection: A Critical Review of the Evidence,"(Columbia University study) *Urban Analysis*, 1979, vol. 6; Peter Kemper and John M. Quigley, *The Economics of Refuse Collection*, (Yale University study) Ballinger, 1976; George E. Peterson, "Pricing and Privatization of Public Services," The Urban Institute, July 1981; E.S. Savas and Barbara Stevens, "The Cost of Residential Refuse Collection and the Effect of Service Arrangement," in *1977 Municipal Year Book*, International City Management Association, 1977.

27. In part, this can be explained by the fact that a government normally would make cost comparisons ahead of time, and if contracting does not seem likely to reduce costs significantly, contracting is not likely to be implemented.

28. John D. Hanrahan, *Government for Sale: Contracting Out the New Patronage*, American Federation of State, County and Municipal Employees, 1977.

29. Shonick and Roemer, "Private Management of California County Hospitals." The study examined seven hospitals with contract management.

30. For example, see Savas, "Intra-city Competition Between Public and Private Service Delivery."

NOTES TO CHAPTER 3

1. The report, Dennis Young, *How Shall We Collect the Garbage?*, The Urban Institute, 1972, has been very helpful in developing this section.

2. The survey was conducted jointly by Columbia University, the International City Management Association, and Public Technology, Inc.. See Savas and Niemczewski, "Who Collects Solid Waste?" *1976 Municipal Yearbook*, International City Management Association, 1976.

3. Citizens League (Minneapolis-St. Paul), minutes of October 28, 1981.

4. Peter Kemper and John M. Quigley, *The Economics of Refuse Collection* Ballinger, 1976; Savas, "Public vs. Private Refuse Collection: A Critical Review of the Evidence;" *Urban Analysis*, 1979, vol. 6; E.S. Savas and Barbara Stevens, *Evaluating the Organization of Service Delivery: Solid Waste Collection and Disposal*, 1976; and George E. Peterson, "The Pricing and Privatization of Public Services." The Urban Institute, July 1981.

5. E.S. Savas, "Policy Analysis for Local Government: Public vs. Private Refuse Collection," *Policy Analysis*, Winter 1977.

6. See Young, *How Shall We Collect the Garbage?*, for further discussion of these points.

7. "Urban Futures Idea Exchange," Vol. 6, No. 9, May 15, 1982.

### NOTES TO CHAPTER 5

1. Robert W. Poole, Jr., *Cutting Back City Hall*, Universe Books, 1980, p. 129.

2. This is advocated in E.G. West, "Choice or Monopoly in Education," *Policy Review*, Winter 1981.

3. Daniel Wieler and others, "A Public School Voucher Demonstration: The First Year at Alum Rock," R-1495-NIE, Rand Corporation, June 1974; and George E. Peterson, "Pricing and Privatization of Public Services," The Urban Institute, July 1981, p. 22. A somewhat earlier and more optimistic view of the demonstration is reported by Denis P. Doyle, "The Alum Rock, California, Education Voucher Project," in *Urban Problems and Public Policy Choices*, ed. Bergsman and Wiener, Praeger, 1975.

4. Poole, *Cutting Back City Hall*, p. 187; and Peterson, "Pricing and Privatization of Public Services," p. 22.

5. The findings are reported in Bernard J. Frieden, "Housing Allowances: An Experiment That Worked," *Public Interest*, Spring 1980; and Raymond Struyk, Mark Bendick, and others, *Housing Vouchers For the Poor: Lessons From a National Experiment*, The Urban Institute Press, 1981.

6. Robert L. Woodson, *A Summons to Life: Mediating Structures in the Prevention of Youth Crime*, Ballinger, 1981; and Poole, *Cutting Back City Hall*, p. 129.

### NOTES TO CHAPTER 6

1. Edwin C. Clay, III, "Why Not Volunteers?" *Virginia Town and City*, December 1978.

2. "Dollar Value of Volunteer Time Estimated at $64.5 Billion," News Release of Independent Sector, Washington, D.C., January 7, 1982.

3. April 29, 1980, memorandum to Mayor and Council from the city manager of the city of Alexandria, Virginia. The city is currently developing a comprehensive plan for the use of volunteers.

4. Arthur Bennet, Jesse Wang, and Lawrence Wasserman, "A Study of the Performance of the Fire Protection System of Montgomery County Maryland," paper for American University, Washington, D.C., 1966.

### NOTES TO CHAPTER 7

1. Adapted from Stuart Langton and James Petersen, "What is Self-Help?" *Citizen Participation*, January/February 1982.

2. These particular examples are also discussed later as examples of "demarketing/reducing the demand" for public services.

3. Citizens League (Minneapolis-St. Paul), minutes of October 28, 1981.

4. *Fiscal Watchdog*, January 1981, Local Government Center, Santa Barbara, California.

5. Many of the concepts discussed here about self-help through neighborhood associations have been adapted from Mark Frazier, "Privatizing the City," *Policy Analysis*, Spring 1980. See also Howard W. Hallman, "Federalism: Make Room for Neighborhoods," *Neighborhoods Ideas*, Civic Action Institute, Washington, D.C., February 1982.

6. Oscar Newman, *Community of Interest*, Anchor Press, 1980, Chap. 6; and *Fiscal Watchdog*, October 1980.

7. *Fiscal Watchdog*, December 1981.

8. JoAnn Ray, "Spokane Police Neighborhood Watch: Year Two Evaluation," Spokane, Washington, February 1974.

9. Midwest Research Institute, "Evaluation of the National Sheriffs' Association Neighborhood Watch Program," Kansas City, Missouri, National Sheriffs' Association, August 10, 1977.

10. Minneapolis-St. Paul, *Citizens League News*, October 7, 1981.

11. See National Sheriffs' Association, "National Neighborhood Watch Program Progress Report," September 23, 1976, p. 5.

## Notes to Chapter 8

1. For this section, the author has made considerable use of materials generated by the Stanford Research Institute's work on "Nonservice Approaches," particularly *Using Non-Service Approaches to Address Neighborhood Problems: A Guide to Local Officials*, Steven A. Waldhorn et al., 1980; and "A Program of Research into Emerging Non-Service Approaches to Social Welfare and Community Development Problems," January 17, 1979. See also "Options to Deal With Public Problems: The Role of Non-Service Approaches," Steven A. Waldhorn statement before the U.S. Senate Subcommittee on Intergovernmental Relations Forum on Alternative Service Delivery, July 28, 1981.

2. *Fiscal Watchdog*, October 1981, Local Government Center, Santa Barbara, California; and Ron Kirby, "The Future of Mass Transit in the United States," *Policy and Research Report*, The Urban Institute, Fall 1981.

3. *Fiscal Watchdog*, March 1981.

4. Citizens League Report, "A Health Care Cost Strategy for the 80's," Minneapolis-St. Paul Citizens League, 1981.

5. See, for example, Robert L. Woodson, *A Summons to Life. Mediating Structures in the Prevention of Youth Crime*, Ballinger, 1981.

## Notes to Chapter 9

1. Citizens League of Minneapolis, Minnesota, "Issues of the 80's: Enlarging Our Capacity to Adapt," August 27, 1980.

2. If the government merely drops an activity without provision for its being picked up by the private sector, this is better considered an extreme example of merely reducing service levels (see "Reduce level of service" under "Other Actions" in exhibit 1).

3. The concepts of mediating structures have been developed by the American Enterprise Institute in a series of reports. See Robert L. Woodson, *A Summons to Life; Mediating Structures and the Prevention of Youth Crime*, Ballinger, 1981; Peter L. Berger and Richard J. Neuhaus, "To Empower People: The Role of Mediating Structures in Public Policy," American Enterprise Institute, 1977; and "The Urban Crisis: Can Grass Roots Groups Succeed Where Government Has Failed?", a forum held May 7, 1981, American Enterprise Institute for Public Policy Research, Washington, D.C.

4. See Woodson, *A Summons to Life*, p. 130.

5. See Michael J. O'Neil, "Issues of Concern to Arizona Families: A Report to the Arizona Delegation to the White House Conference on Families," and its summary, "Family Concerns and Institutional Preferences of Arizona Citizens," Arizona's Governor's Council on Children, Youth and Families, June 1980.

6. Woodson, *A Summons to Life*, p. 133–138.

7. Mark Frazier, "Transatlantic Perspectives," German Marshall Fund.

8. Statement of William G. White, Hospital Corporation of America, before the U.S. Senate Subcommittee on Intergovernmental Relations, Forum on Alternative Service Delivery, July 29, 1981.

9. Materials provided by Prince George's County, Budget Office.

10. William Shonick and Ruth Roemer, "Private Management of California County Hospitals," School of Public Health, University of California, Los Angeles, paper presented at the American Public Health Association meeting, Detroit, Michigan, October 19, 1980, p. 5.

11. Ibid., p. 7.

12. *Hospital Statistics*, American Hospital Association, 1980.

13. E. Richard Brown, "Public Hospitals and Prices: Their Problems and Their Options," School of Public Health, University of California at Los Angeles, February 1981. Brown's information is from James M. Cameron and Joseph H. Hafkenschiel, "Using DRGs and CHFC Data to Describe Differences in Hospital Costs," paper presented at the California Health Facilities Commission, Third Annual Symposium, Monterey, California, May 1, 1980.

14. George E. Peterson, "Pricing and Privatization of Public Services, The Urban Institute, July 1981." pp. 18–19.

15. Ibid.

16. Woodson, *A Summons to Life*, and Robert L. Woodson's presentation at the U.S. Senate Subcommittee on Intergovernmental Relations Forum on Alternative Service Delivery, July 29, 1981.

17. American Enterprise Institute, "The Urban Crisis: Can Grass Roots Groups Succeed Where Government Has Failed?"

18. Bruce McKinnon and Sean Sullivan, "Private Sector Initiatives: Selected Examples," The American Enterprise Institute, December 1981.

19. Harold Wohlman and George E. Peterson, "State and Local Government Strategies for Responding to Fiscal Pressure," *Tulane Law Review*, April 1981, p. 793.

20. Peterson, "Pricing and Privatization of Public Services," p. 19.

21. See E.S. Savas, "Public vs. Private Refuse Collection: A Critical Review of the Evidence," *Urban Analysis* 1979, vol. 6; Peter Kemper and John M. Quigley, *The Economics of Refuse Collection*, Ballinger, 1976; and George E. Peterson, "Pricing and Privatization of Public Services."

NOTES TO CHAPTER 10

1. Prince George's County, *Annual Productivity and Improvement and Cost Reduction Plan*, April 1981.

2. Charles Brecker and Raymond D. Horton, eds., *Setting Municipal Priorities, 1982*, Russell Sage Foundation, New York, 1982, p. 255.

NOTES TO CHAPTER 11

1. These examples were reported in the *Public Administration Times*, February 1, 1981, p. 12; and "Cost Cutting Strategies for the Park and Recreation Agency," U.S. Department of Interior, Park and Recreation Technical Services, 1981, p. 40.

2. "Cost Cutting Strategies for the Park and Recreation Agency," p. 40.

3. "Public-Private Partnership: An Opportunity for Urban Communities," Committee For Economic Development, Washington, D.C. February 1982, p. 70.

4. *The Washington Post*, August 12, 1981, p. D8.

5. Prince George's County, *Annual Productivity and Improvement and Cost Reduction Plan*, April 1981.

6. "Public-Private Partnership: An Opportunity for Urban Communities," Committee for Economic Development, Washington, D.C., February 1982, pp. 67–68.

### NOTES TO CHAPTER 12

1. The paper by Paul B. Downing, "User Charges and Service Fees: An Information Bulletin for the Urban Consortium," U.S. Department of Housing and Urban Development, Office of Policy Development and Research, 1981, has been very useful in preparing this chapter.

2. For example, while total revenues for cities and counties increased at an annual rate of 9.6% between FY 1977 and FY 1981, revenues from charges increased at the annual rate of 13.9% (derived from figures from table 1 of *City Government Finances in 1980–81*, GF81 No. 4, and *County Government Finances in 1980–81*, GF81 No. 8, both U.S. Bureau of the Census reports, December 1982). Survey by the Advisory Commission on Intergovernmental Relations (ACIR) and the Municipal Finance Officers Association found that 77.5 percent of the 307 responding cities reported increased use of user charges over the period 1980–1982; 25.1 percent reported increased use of special assessments, ACIR, February 10, 1982.

3. Frazier, "Transatlantic Perspectives," German Marshall Fund.

4. Michael Fix, "The Impact of Regulation on Housing Costs: Snohomish County Case Study," The Urban Institute, February 1982, draft.

5. Downing, "User Charges and Service Fees," pp. 21–23.

6. Fees and charges may be less fair to apartment dwellers living in apartments that provide privately for services such as waste collection. Apartment dwellers may pay through their rent both for property taxes and the private service (unless the government has adjusted the taxes accordingly).

7. Downing, "User Charges and Fees," p. 23.

8. "1981 Changing Public Attitudes on Governments and Taxes," S-10, ACIR, Washington, D.C. 1982.

9. Data from ACIR-MFOA, December 1981 survey, February 10, 1982.

### NOTE TO CHAPTER 13

1. Another set of ratings of alternative service delivery approaches is given in the recently published work, E.S. Savas, *Privatizing the Public Sector: How to Shrink Government*, Chatham House Publications, Inc. 1982, Chap. 5.